FREE BOOKS

www.forgottenbooks.org

You can read literally <u>thousands</u> of books
for free at www.forgottenbooks.org

(please support us by visiting our web site)

Truth may seem, but cannot be:
Beauty brag, but 'tis not she;
Truth and beauty buried be.

To this urn let those repair
That are either true or fair;
For these dead birds sigh a prayer.

Bacon

Launching the Airship.

THE BOYS' BOOK OF MODEL AEROPLANES

HOW TO BUILD AND FLY THEM: WITH THE STORY OF THE EVOLUTION OF THE FLYING MACHINE

BY

FRANCIS A. COLLINS

ILLUSTRATED WITH MANY
PHOTOGRAPHS AND DIAGRAMS·
BY THE AUTHOR

NEW YORK
THE CENTURY CO.
1910

TO

ARNOLD MILLER COLLINS
(Aged Ten)

THAN WHOM NO COLLABORATOR COULD
HAVE BEEN MORE ENTHUSIASTIC

CONTENTS

PART I

MODELS: HOW TO BUILD AND FLY THEM

PART II

THE HISTORY AND SCIENCE OF AVIATION

LIST OF ILLUSTRATIONS

LIST OF ILLUSTRATIONS

LIST OF ILLUSTRATIONS

PART I

MODELS: HOW TO BUILD AND FLY THEM

THE BOYS' BOOK OF MODEL AEROPLANES

CHAPTER I

THE NEW SPORT FOR BOYS

IN the boy's calendar nowadays the aëroplane season comes in with sledding and runs all through skating, marble, top, kite-flying, and bicycle time. The delights of all the old games seem to be found in this marvelous new toy. The fun in throwing a top cannot compare with that of launching an aëroplane, while kite-flying is a very poor substitute for the actual conquest of the air. To watch one of these fascinating little ships of the air, which you have fashioned and built with your own hands, actually rise from the earth and soar aloft with a swallow's swiftness, is perhaps the greatest boy's sport in the world. Certainly no new game or toy has ever taken such hold of the boy's imagination, and in so short a time enrolled such an army of enthusiasts.

Throughout the country to-day upward of ten thousand boy aviators are struggling with the problem of the air-ship. Among these junior aëronauts the record for height and that for distance in flying are matters of quite as lively interest as among the grown-ups. The great contests of aviators here and abroad are watched with intelligent interest. Let a new form of aëroplane, a biplane or monoplane, appear, and it is quickly reproduced by scores of models and its virtues put to an actual test. If a new wing or new plan for insuring stability is invented, a new thought in the steering-device, or some new application of power, it is instantly the subject of earnest discussion among the junior aëronauts the country over.

Nor are junior aëronauts merely imitators. The mystery of the problems of the air, the fascination of a new world of conquest, make a strong appeal to the American temperament. With thousands of bright boys working with might and main to build air-ships which will actually fly, there is certain to be real progress. Thousands of different models have been designed and put to actual test. This army of inventors, ranging in age from twelve to eighteen years, some of whom will be the aviators of the future, cannot fail to do great service, as time goes on, in the actual conquest of the air.

Within a few months this army of inventors has become organized into clubs, and a regular program of tournaments has been arranged. The junior aëro clubs are found in connection with many schools, both public and private; they are made features of the Young Men's Christian Association amusements, or they become identified with various neighborhoods. Tournaments are arranged between clubs of different cities or States, while an international tournament is even planned between the United States and Great Britain.

The junior aëro world has its prizes, which are scarcely less coveted than the rewards for actual flight. Some fifty medals have been distributed this year among the members of the New York Junior Aëro Club. Many elaborate trophies will be contended for during 1910 by the junior aëronauts of the country. A handsome silver cup of special design has been presented by Mr. A. Leo Stevens, and a second by Mr. Sidney Bowman, while similar trophies are offered by Commodore Marshall, O. Chanute, and others.

The toy aëroplane is not limited to any one season, as one's sled, kite, or skates. In the winter months the tests of flight may be carried out in any large room or hall. There is even an advantage in holding such a tournament in a large schoolroom, riding-academy, or armory, since there is no baffling wind to contend with. Already definite rules have been laid down for conducting these tests and for making

A Junior Aëroclub with Its Instructor in One of the New York Public Schools.

official records of flights. It is possible, therefore, to compare the records made in different cities or countries with one another.

The junior aëro tournaments are likely to be the most thrilling experience in a boy's life. The feats which the world has watched with such breathless interest at aviation meets at Rheims, Pau, or Los Angeles are reproduced in miniature in these boys' contests without loss of enthusiasm. The weeks or months of preparation in scores of little workshops are now put to an actual test. The model air-ship, which has cost so many anxious and delightful hours in the building, is to spread its wings with scores of similar air-craft. The superiority of the monoplane or biplane forms is to be tested without fear or favor.

For the young inventors, even for the mere layman in such matters, the scene is extremely animated. On every hand one sees the inventors tuning up their air-craft for the final test. There are lively discussions in progress over the marvelous little toys. The layman hears a new language spoken with perfect confidence about him. The boys have already made the picturesque vocabulary of the world of aviation their own. The discussion ranges over monoplanes and biplanes, cellular types, and flexed planes, or of rigid and lateral braces. To hear a crowd of these enthusiasts shout their comments as the air-ships fly about is in itself an education in advanced aëronautics.

Directly the floor is cleared, the judges take their position, and the junior sky-pilot toes the mark, air-ship in hand. "One, two, three," shouts the starter, and with a whir the graceful air-craft is launched. The flutter of the tiny propeller suggests the sudden rise of a covey of partridges. The little craft, at once so graceful and frail, defies all the accepted laws of gravitation. It darts ahead in long, undulating curves as it floats over the invisible air-currents. As in the aëroplanes of larger size, the length of the flight is dependent almost wholly on the motive power. As the little engine slows down, the craft wavers, and then in a long curve, for it can do nothing ungraceful, it glides to rest, skidding along the floor like a bird reluctant to leave the sky.

When the time comes for the races between the air-craft, enthusiasm runs high. Naturally these contests are the most popular features of the tournament. A line of inventors, with their air-craft, usually six at a time, take their positions at the starting-line. Each air-craft has been tuned to its highest powers. The labor of weeks, the study of air-craft problems, the elaboration of pet inventive schemes, are represented in the shining model. And the problem before the young inventors is most baffling. There are few models to work from, the science is still so young, and the inventor may well feel himself something of a Columbus in launching his frail craft upon this uncharted sea.

At the signal half a dozen propellers are instantly released, a whirring as of innumerable light wings fills the air. The curious flock of mechanical birds rises and falls, dipping in long, graceful curves as they struggle toward the goal. Some graceful little craft perfectly reproducing to the last detail the famous Wright machine shoulders along beside a glistening monoplane which resembles a great hawk with wings outspread. The next craft is perhaps a complicated arrangement of planes of no registered type, while the craft made familiar by the photographs of the famous aviators are reproduced.

The thrill of an aëroplane race is a sensation peculiarly its own. It seems so astonishing that the graceful little craft should remain aloft at all, that they are a never-failing delight to the eye. The varying fortunes of the race, the temporary lead gained by one craft, to be lost the next moment to another, which a second later itself falls behind, and the final heat between the survivors in the race as they approach the goal, are enough to drive the average boy crazy with delight.

A Young Inventor in His Workshop.

Boys Comparing Models.

The rules for these contests are rigidly observed. Each air-craft is sent aloft by its inventor or owner. The start must be made from a mark, and of course each aëroplane must toe the mark. There must be three judges for each event. One stands at the starting-line and gives the word of command for the start of the race or flight, as the case may be. A second judge stands midway down the course, and the third at or near the finishing-line. Each young aviator winds up his craft, adjusts the power with his own hands, and sets the rudder for the flight.

The miniature air-craft must act in flight exactly the same as the great working air-craft which carry men aloft. A toy air-ship must make its flight in a horizontal position, and if it turns over in flight, even though it flies farther and faster than any other, it is disqualified. The craft must also fly in a reasonably straight line toward the goal, and should it be deflected for any reason and go off at a tangent, the flight, no matter how successful otherwise,

will not be counted. In case of a collision
between air-craft, the race is repeated.
The responsibility for adjusting the
power, arranging the steering-gear, and
giving direction to the flight at the start
is entirely in the hands of the young engineer himself.

In measuring the length of the flights,
again, the point at which the air-ship first
touches the ground is fixed arbitrarily as
the end. Often the little craft merely
grazes the ground to rise and skid for
many feet, but in the official count this
secondary flight is not considered. First
and last, no one but the owner of the little
craft is permitted to touch it. The grace
with which the ship lands is also taken
into consideration in granting the prizes.
Each boy is permitted three trials. As in
the regular aviation world, these records
rarely stand for more than a few days at
a time.

These air-ships are driven by ropes of
rubber bands which are turned on themselves until they are tightly knotted, when

in unwinding they serve to drive the propeller around some hundreds of times. The rubber is so light that it adds little to the weight of the craft. The motor is of course a makeshift and at best only serves to keep the propeller in motion for a fraction of a minute. Experiments have been made in driving the propeller with compressed air, which is carried in an aluminium rod fastened beneath the planes. But the force of thousands of youthful inventive geniuses is certain to bring forth some new motive power.

It is characteristic of the American boy that our young aviators should feel themselves disgraced to fly a model not of their own make. As a result, miniature craft of amazing ingenuity and workmanship are being turned out by the amateur aviators all over the country. The materials employed, such as rattan, bamboo, or light lath, and the silk for covering the planes, or the wires for bracing the frame, cost but a few pennies. Toy aviation is one of the most democratic of sports.

CHAPTER II

THE aviator must venture in his frail craft upon an unknown and uncharted sea. The great problem is to ride the shifting air currents and keep the machine right side up. Although we cannot see the air currents, we know that they are constantly ebbing and flowing, piling themselves in great heaps, or slipping away in giddy vortices. There is much beautiful scenery, high mountain peaks, deep valleys, and level plains formed by these ever shifting air currents through which the aviator must steer his course blindly as best he may. A great bank of whirling clouds driven before the wind shows how rough and tumbling a sea he must navigate.

The air being a much thinner medium

than water is, of course, far more unstable and baffling. Its supporting power is not only very small but constantly varies. The flying machine which will navigate successfully in a perfectly quiet atmosphere may be unseaworthy, or rather, unairworthy, when a wind springs up, or the shifting of the wind may spoil all the air pilot's plans. To add to his troubles, the aviator must move among air currents which change and change again in a moment's time. As we study the difficulties of air navigation we will appreciate, more than ever, the wonderful patience, skill, and daring of the successful aviators.

The action of the air currents had first to be carefully studied before flight became possible. Although the air is invisible we now know exactly how the air currents act upon the wings or planes. When a plane surface, such as the wing of an aëroplane, moves horizontally through the air, the air is caught for a moment underneath it and is pressed down slightly and a moment later slips out again from under the other edges at the sides and back. It is this air under pressure which yields a slight support.

It has been proven by many experiments that this supporting power varies with the shape of the plane or surface driven horizontally through the air. A long narrow surface driven sideways gains much more support from the air than the same area in the form of a square or any other shape. In other words, a square surface ten feet square containing 100 square feet will not travel as far as a surface twenty feet long and five feet wide.

The explanation is very simple. As the square surface moves along, the air is momentarily compressed under the front edge, but instantly slips off at the back and sides. As the broad surface of the rectangular plane cuts the air, however, few of the air currents can escape at the sides while the most of them are crowded together and held in place until they slip off at the back. The supporting power of the plane is therefore in direct proportion to the length of the front or, as it is called, the entering edge of the plane.

Here we find one of the secrets of the flight of birds. The spread between the tips of their outstretched wings is much greater than the width of the wings themselves. It also explains why the Wright model, for instance, should be so oddly shaped and should move sideways like a crab. If you study the models of the successful monoplanes with this in mind they have a new meaning. The law of the proportion of the entering edge is very important in designing an aëroplane.

It is so important for the air to be confined as long as possible beneath the gliding plane that many devices have been tried to hold it. Some planes are built with a slight edge running around the sides and back, on the under surface, to hem in the air. Some of the biplanes are built with closed sides, the cellular form they are called, to keep the air from slipping away. The box kite is constructed with this in view. The builder of model aëroplanes will find, however, that the slight edge formed by turning the cloth over the frame of the plane is sufficient to hold the air.

The flight of a kite, by the way, appears a very simple matter once this law is understood. The air currents strike the kite at an angle and are deflected or carrom off at exactly the same angle. A line drawn through the middle of this angle, exactly bisecting it, will give you the direction of the force exerted by the wind. Meanwhile the kite string holds the plane rigidly in position. As the kite darts from side to side it is merely obeying this law and adjusting itself so that its surface will stand at right angles to this thrust of the wind. An aëroplane is simply a kite which makes its own wind or air currents.

The kite is, of course, balanced against the wind currents and kept more or less stable by its cord, but an aëroplane must balance itself. The secret of insuring stability was discovered only after years of experience with gliders in actual flights.

The stability of the aëroplane depends upon the proper adjustment of the pressure of the air on the machine. There is, of course, a center of pressure, just as there is a center of gravity in every aëroplane of whatever form or size. It may be laid down as a general rule that a plane traveling horizontally in a quiet atmosphere is kept horizontal and stable by making the centers of pressure and gravity coincide.

The air currents, as we pointed out, are never entirely at rest but are constantly tilting the plane about. Hold a sheet of stiff paper horizontally and let it fall. It will flutter to the ground or perhaps be twirled away, indicating the presence of a number of unexpected air currents. The aëroplane which would remain stable in a perfectly quiet atmosphere must overcome all these twists and turns. The problem of stability has not yet of course been solved. Having reached this stage in the evolution of the aëroplane the aviator next began to experiment by bending his wings or planes and throwing out lateral or stability planes to help him keep his balance.

It was now found that a very little tilting of the planes upward or downward would serve to right the machine when it leaned over. The secret, like so many others, was gained by watching the flights of birds. You have perhaps seen a great albatross or sea gull soar without the slightest effort and apparently without motion. Look more closely and you will see that the tips of the broad wings move slightly from time to time, while the main body of the wings remains rigid, which is the great secret of stability in flight.

The ends of the planes were next made flexible, very slightly so, and arranged so that they might be moved up and down or flexed at will. The flights made with this adjustment were at once brought under control. New planes were added before and behind, and it was found that the machine could be kept from darting up and down just as well as tilting over at the ends. The aëroplane was now ready for the installation of the motor.

The best curve for the wing of an aëroplane is an irregular curve drawn above the horizontal line. It is not a perfect arc of a circle but reaches its greatest height about one third back of the front edge, with the rest of the line slightly flattened. It is much the same line as is formed by some waves just before they break. The plane thus shaped is driven with the blunt or entering edge forward or against the wind. In building the large aëroplanes this curve is worked out with great accuracy, but the builder of model airships may carry the line in his eye.

As the air strikes the entering edge of this surface it is driven underneath and held there for a moment before it can escape from beneath this hollow. The support of the air is therefore greater than in the case of a flat plane, or in fact, any other form. The air which passes over the top of the entering edge, meanwhile, glides or slips off at a slight upward angle, thus forming a partial vacuum over the greater part of the upper surface. This vacuum, in turn, tends to pull the plane slightly upward thus acting in the same direction as the air which is compressed beneath it.

The planes thus constructed are, besides, much more easily controlled than those of any other shape. When the entering edge of this plane is raised the pressure of the air beneath is increased and the pull of the partial vacuum combines with it to make it rise. The difficult problem of getting the aëroplane aloft was largely solved by this curve. Once aloft, such an airship answers her helm much better than any other form.

This curve is accountable for many of the movements of aëroplanes which seem so mysterious to the mere layman. When an aëroplane turns, its outer end rises, and the more rapid is its flight the greater is this tilt. It must be remembered that the end is moving more rapidly and the increased speed causes the plane to lift. Many photographs of aëroplanes show

The First Glider Weighted at the Front.

them balanced at precarious angles while making a turn. If the plane is tilted too high the air currents slip out from beneath, no vacuum is developed above, and it quickly loses speed. On the other hand, if it be inclined downward it soon loses the supporting power of the air and plunges down.

At every stage of this development the aviators are indebted to the birds for information. The successful aëroplanes have great width compared to their depth, they gain stability by flexing the tips of the wings, and their planes are arched upward and forward exactly as are the wings of a bird. The aviator arranges his center of gravity after the same general model, below the planes and well forward. He places his engine forward, just as the bird has its strongest muscles in the chest, and he builds his frame of hollow tubes like the bones of a bird.

CHAPTER III

HOW TO BUILD A "GLIDER"

THE simplest form of heavier-than-air machine is the stiff card or letter which you may spin across the room. If you give it just the right twirl it will glide on a level for many feet. There are many ways besides of folding a sheet of stiff paper which will convert it into a surprisingly clever little airship. With a little practice these gliders may be made to fly ten or twenty times their own length, which would be a very creditable flight for the best aëroplane models.

There is no better way to begin the construction of a model aëroplane than by study and experiment with these paper ships. The most famous aëronauts of the day, the Wright brothers, Curtiss, Herring, and many others, have spent years working with gliders before attempting to build or fly an aëroplane. It is in this way that they discovered what form of wing would support the greatest weight, whether the passenger should stand up or lie down, how to place the propeller and the rudder, and hundreds of other details which have made possible the actual conquests of the air.

Following in their footsteps, or rather their flights, the amateur aëronaut should first build and fly only gliders or aëroplanes without means of self-propulsion. The simplest form of glider may be made by cutting a broad oval from a sheet of stiff letter-paper and creasing it down the middle. The experiment may be made more interesting, however, by cutting out the plane like the outstretched wings of a bird, as suggested in the accompanying illustration. Try as you may, this sheet will not fly. Now add a trifling weight to the front of the plane. This may be done by fastening one or more paper clips to the edge, pasting a match or a toothpick, or by dropping a little tallow or sealing-wax.

At first you will underestimate the weight your little airship will carry. Add more weight in the same way, and test its gliding powers until the little airship will glide gracefully across the floor. Keep the length of these models under six inches. If you increase it beyond this, the model loses steadiness and flutters about ineffectively.

An interesting model may be made by folding a sheet of stiff paper in an arrow-like form. The idea is to form a series of planes which will support the weight of the tiny craft and, at the same time, enable it to fly or dart in a straight line. It will be found that the vertical surfaces lend stability and keep the ship moving in a straight line. You will soon learn, in this way, more of the principles of aëroplane construction than mere reading from books can teach you. Be careful, meanwhile, to remember just how you have launched the various forms of models,

Dowel Strips of Different Sizes.

whether you have thrown them with an upward or downward motion, and how hard a push you have given them. The skill you acquire in this way will be valuable later on when you come to launch your regular model aëroplane.

We are now ready to begin the construction of the frames of aëroplane models. The first model will be merely a glider. The frame and wings or planes of an aëroplane are built much the same as a kite. The idea in all such work is to combine the greatest possible strength or stability with extreme lightness. Remember, however, that the aëroplane during its flights is racked and shaken by its motor, and is likely to land with a bump. The materials used must be stronger than in the case of an ordinary kite, the joints more securely formed, and the entire structure braced in every possible way.

The best materials for constructing these gliders or aëroplanes are very cheap and easily obtained. At almost any hardware-store you will find a variety of "dowel-sticks," which seem especially made for this work. They are smooth, round sticks a yard in length and of a variety of diameter. The sticks three sixteenths of an inch in diameter will be found most serviceable, while the larger sticks are just the thing for the backbones of your aëroplane. These sticks will not split at the ends and may be readily worked. They cost one cent apiece.

Some boys find that the reed or cane suits their purpose better than the dowel-sticks, since it is more flexible and a trifle lighter. The cane is easy to work when you wish to build planes with curved lines. It can be readily shaped to any desired form by first wetting it and allowing it to dry after working. Care must be taken in using it, since the ends are likely to split. Bundles of this cane may be bought at most hardware-stores or in department-stores. Enough material for constructing a model may be bought for a few cents.

The lightest of all available materials is bamboo. It is difficult to procure, how-

Care must be taken to have the sides of the rectangle exactly the same length and the joints closely and neatly finished. Some boys prefer to lay one stick over another, then wrap the joint tightly with thin but strong linen thread, and over this brush a coat of thin glue, without using any brads or nails.

In kite-building, to be sure, it would be enough to lay the strips over one another and fasten roughly with a tack. Nor did the lengths of the stick, when covered with paper, make much if any difference. The aëroplane, it must be remembered, travels edgewise, and, having no guiding string, is at the mercy of every gust of wind. If the frames are carelessly proportioned it will not travel true, but is likely to be deflected. Imagine a boat whose sides are not exactly uniform trying to travel in a straight line. It would be lopsided, and would roll and pitch under the most favorable conditions. Now an aëroplane, since it travels in so thin a medium as air, is far more sensitive than a boat, and it becomes lopsided if its proportions be in the least inaccurate. Only the greatest care in construction will produce an air craft which will fly true and straight.

It makes little or no difference in a kite if the ends project a little and the joints be carelessly made. Not only must your aëroplane be perfectly proportioned, but it must be finished like a piece of fine furniture. The question of friction is a very important one in the heavier-than-air machine. You cannot be too careful to round off every corner and smooth every exposed surface. If you have opportunity to see a regular aëroplane, a Wright or Curtiss model, you will find that every part of the machine has been sandpapered and varnished with the greatest care. This is not done for the sake of appearances, but because it has been found that the wind striking against the rough piece of wood meets an appreciable amount of resistance, whereas it slips past a polished surface with little or no friction. Your aëroplane should be finished like a violin.

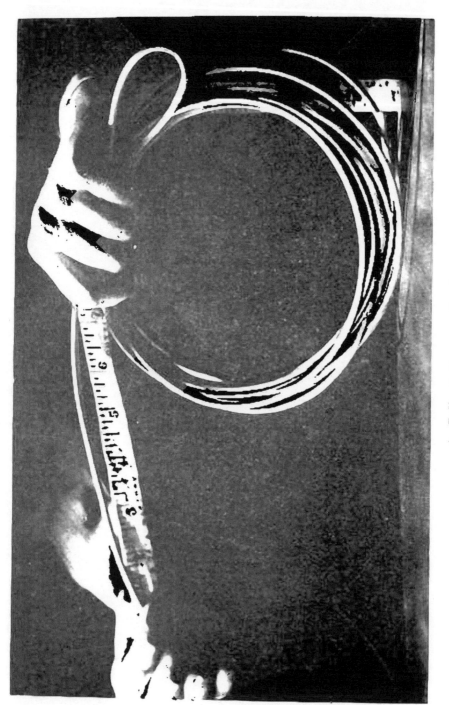

A Coil of Cane or Reed.

HOW TO BUILD A "GLIDER"

In building these planes be careful to compare the lengths of the corresponding sides throughout. If you prefer to use brads for fastening the joints do so. The dowel-stick and bamboo will take the brads with little danger of splitting. When thoroughly dry, cut away the glue which has squeezed out, round off the ends, and sandpaper with fine sand or emery-paper. If you use brads it will not be necessary to place the joints in a vise while drying. Should your strips split, bore the holes with a fine awl. Some boys after drilling the holes merely tie and glue the sticks together, using no nails whatever.

Now cut three dowel-strips 34 inches long and slightly sharpen their ends, so that when brought together they will form a prism whose base is about one fourth their length. Next bend a strong piece of wire into a hook — a hair-pin will answer for small models — and fasten it in the apex of the prism, with the hook inside. The projecting end of wire should then be bent over, and the three dowel-sticks glued and tied tightly together.

At the open end of the prism next fasten two strips from end to end, leaving the third side of the triangle open. Now fasten your two planes on the open side of the prism, slightly mortising the sticks and gluing and nailing them securely in position. To further strengthen the prism, join the three sides at the middle with three sticks, forming a complete triangle. The prism thus braced will be found as strong as a heavy central stick, besides being much lighter and providing an excellent base for the propeller. A strong stick about half an inch square should be tied and glued across the middle of the triangle at the base of the prism to support the motor.

The frame once complete, sandpapered and varnished, it is ready to be covered. At first this may be done with some smooth paper. Almost any thin material, muslin or linen, will answer for the purpose, although white silk makes the most finished-looking model. Such scraps as may be found in the family piece-bag will answer every purpose. In sewing the cloth over the frame the advice of some big sister, aunt, or the mother may well be taken. The idea is to fasten the cloth smoothly and neatly over the frame, keeping the surface free from creases or wrinkles of any kind. Boys are likely to be awkward with the needle. The cloth may also be glued over the frames. When complete cover the planes with a thin solution of paraffin dissolved in benzine.

In attaching the planes or wings to the central axis of the model, the larger stick or backbone may be mortised neatly, so that the sides of the frame will be sunk in flush with the upper surface. A fairly good glider may be made, however, by merely nailing down the frames against this backbone. The distance between the two planes is a complicated problem, but the beginner had better at first imitate the model shown in the accompanying illustration. If the two supporting planes be too far apart or too near together, the glider will fall. The amateur must experiment by changing their position on the central axis until he hits the right proportion. He will be able later to carry this proportion in his eye, and the experience will prove invaluable. Until you have hit upon the proper position, fasten them to the backbone with rubber bands. These permit you to slide the planes back and forth without the trouble of nailing.

Aëroplanes, unlike kites, fly best in a perfectly quiet atmosphere. If you make your trial flights out of doors, select a quiet day. A room, a barn, or any large interior will be found better. In launching your glider, hold it from beneath, so that it balances, and throw it forward with a swift, steady movement of the arm. A little practice will make you very expert.

You will now find yourself fitted to reproduce any of the simpler forms of monoplane models, several of which are here illustrated. An interesting model is made by attaching U-shaped wings to a central

Splitting a Bamboo Fish-Pole.

axis. In making these curved planes the reed will be found useful. Other effective gliders are made with triangular wings fixed at a variety of angles. Remember that the model must be absolutely symmetrical. In attaching the frames to the central axis, always make the joints as smooth and rigid as possible.

The weighting of the glider will be found to be a very important detail. As a rule the gliders require a considerable weight at the front. The exact position of the weight can only be determined by experiment. The simplest way is to wire a nail or a piece of metal to the edge of the frame. If your glider does not balance perfectly, which is likely to be the case, this fault can be largely remedied by weighting it. The tendency of the glider is likely to be upward, and the weight serves to keep it on an even keel. When your model glides steadily through the air, without rolling or pitching, you have constructed a well-balanced frame. It will then be time to take up the problem of propulsion.

CHAPTER IV

A WELL-CONSTRUCTED glider alone makes a fascinating toy, but once the motor has been installed it seems almost alive. Your little craft will now be ready for new conquests. It will imitate the flights of the famous aviators, contending with the same problems, perhaps meeting similar accidents.

The motor is the most interesting, as it is the most important, detail of the aëroplane. Although it is possible to buy the propellers for the motor, it is advisable that every boy should work out this problem for himself. An effective motor is easy to build, and costs practically nothing. The length of your propeller-blades should be equal to about one third the width of your largest plane. For this you will need six strips of some light wood, such as pine or ash, although a cigar-box wood, if the grain be straight, will answer. Cut the strips to measure about half an inch in width and one eighth of an inch thick. (See Plate B.)

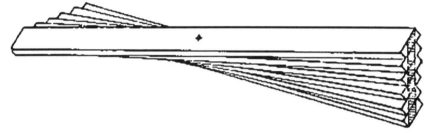

THE PROPELLER BEFORE CUTTING DOWN.

PLATE B.

The strips should be covered with a thin glue and laid one on top of another, and a very thin nail be carefully driven through the little pile at the exact center between the two ends. While the glue is still soft, turn the sticks on the axis formed by the nail, so that they make a double fan, spacing the outer edges about one quarter of an inch apart. Be certain that the fan is regular, and then give the nail a final rap to tighten its hold and keep all the glued surfaces together, and set away to dry. If you can prop up the ends it will be better to put a flat-iron or other weight on each end to make the strips glue together tighter.

The thrust or propelling power depends as much upon the curves of the propeller as upon the force with which the motor is driven. If the propeller be too flat, it will not take hold of the air, while if the pitch or angle of the curve be too sharp, it will simply bore holes in the air and create a vacuum which is useless. The pitch should be about one in twelve; that is, if the propeller-blade be twelve inches long, the curve should be one inch high.

When the glue is thoroughly dry and hard the projecting step-like edges may be cut away. A flat chisel or an ordinary pen-knife will do the work. Be careful to keep the ends uniform, since much depends upon the balance. Cut away the wood until the blades are one eighth of an inch or less in thickness, and round off the corners. The propeller should then be sandpapered perfectly smooth and varnished. You will be delighted to find how professional and shipshape the finished propeller will be.

Now carefully remove the nail fastening the pieces, and you will find, of course, that it marks the exact center and forms a perfect axis. Should you need to enlarge this hole, do not attempt to bore it, since this may split the wood, but burn it out, using a nail heated over a gas-flame. Now insert a stiff wire in this hole — a hat-pin will answer — and fasten it by clenching it at the back tight to the propeller, and fill up the hole with glue. The photographs of the propellers of various models will give you an excellent idea of the proper curve.

Aviators differ as to the proper position for the propellers in toy aëroplanes. Here is a problem you must work out for yourself. Some believe that the propeller placed in front of the planes gets a firmer grip on the air, since when the propeller is at the stern the planes make many disturbing currents, just as a steamship churns the water in its wake. Others argue that by placing this propelling force at the rear of the planes the craft is made more steady. At any rate, excellent flights may be made with either arrangement.

In connecting up your propeller with the motor it is very important that the shaft should turn freely and that the bearings offer the least possible resistance. If you have built your aëroplane from the drawing (see Plate A), now drill a hole exactly in the center of the stick which crosses the triangle at the rear of the frame. This hole will come on a line with the apex of the prism, or exactly in the center of the triangle. When the turning of the motor pulls the ends of the frame together, the strain will therefore be exactly distributed among the three sides or braces.

The propeller must be kept clear of the frame and must never touch or scrape against it. First a thin strip of metal, drilled to take the axle or hat-pin, should be nailed over the hole in the crosspiece. A sheet of aluminium such as is used for name-plates is just the thing. Now on the propeller-wire or axis string a smooth, symmetrical glass bead, and pass the axle through the metal strip and the crosspiece. This will give you an excellent substitute for ball-bearings. The end of the wire should then be turned into a hook well inside the frame. The propeller should be mounted so carefully that it will turn freely without friction and without wabbling from side to side.

The simplest and most effective motor is formed by connecting the two hooks with many turns of a long, thin strand of rubber, which can be bought by the yard or pound. The thinner strands of rubber will exert more force than the heavy bands, and red rubber is more durable than any other. The bands should be looped loosely between the two hooks, just as you would wind a skein of zephyr — over the hook on the propeller-"shaft," then around the hook at the other end, then down over the propeller-shaft hook, and so on. If the hooks be three feet apart the combined strands should form a band one inch or more in diameter. If you cannot buy the rubber in this form, a number of two-inch rubber bands, such as you buy by the box at the stationer's, may be lopped chain fashion together to form a continuous rope from hook to hook.

To store up energy for the flight, simply turn your propeller round and round until the rope of rubber bands is tightly knotted. You can readily tell when it is sufficiently wound and the danger-point is reached, which comes when the pull of the rubber grows too strong for your frame. The average motor should be turned about one hundred and fifty times. When the propeller is released the rubber bands in unwinding will give you back almost exactly the same number of revolutions, less perhaps one or two, which represents the loss through friction.

If the propeller simply buzzes around, coming to rest in a few seconds, without

Model Constructed from Diagram, Plate A.

raising your aëroplane, it is probably too small for the weight of the aëroplane. When fully wound up the propeller should run for about ten seconds. On the other hand, if the propeller be too large, it will quickly twist the aëroplane out of its course and drive it to earth. It is well to try out your motor thoroughly to make sure of its running smoothly before attempting any actual flights.

Do not yield to the temptation of trying your wings, however, until the skids have been attached. Most of the regular full-size aëroplanes run on ordinary bicycle wheels, although the Wrights use runners like a sleigh. These skids or runners enable the machine to run along the ground with the least possible friction and greatly assist in rising. In the models of aëroplanes the skids serve a double purpose in protecting the machine when it alights.

A serviceable ˌskid may be made by building a triangle of thin strips and attaching it to the frame with the broad side downward, as shown in the accompanying drawing. Skids made of reed curving down from the main body of the aëroplane will also serve to take up the shock. There are many ways of constructing these skids, and a study of the models here illustrated will give many suggestions. If you intend to have your aëroplane start from the ground, the front skids should be somewhat longer than those in the rear to give it the proper lift.

The friction of the skids is greatly reduced by mounting them on wheels. Small metal wheels may be borrowed from toy automobiles, or small disks of wood or cork will answer for the purpose. A very simple axis may be formed by running a long hat-pin through the uprights of the skids. The photographs of the best models will be found full of suggestions. You will need at least three skids to form a tripod for your aëroplane. It makes little difference if you use one leg in front, or two.

It is very important that the frame should be properly braced to withstand the strain brought upon it. In the glider this bracing is less important, but the action of the motor changes the situation. The rapid movement of the propellers wracks the entire frame, and the impact on landing is naturally greater when the weight is increased. A thin copper wire, No. 32, 34, or 36, should be used, which will be found strong and flexible, while adding little to the weight. After constructing your aëroplane go over it carefully and cut away the wood wherever it may be lightened, and then strengthen it by bracing. Wherever a joint may be strengthened or a strut or a plane be made more rigid by bracing, do not spare the wire.

The accompanying drawing, with the photographs of models, will indicate how these braces may best be applied. To begin with, braces should be run, wherever possible, from the corners of the planes to the central frame and the skids. In the monoplane forms you will find it worth while to add posts or perpendiculars to the upper side of the frame and run wire braces diagonally to the ends of the planes. The extreme ends of the planes should also be connected.

No matter how carefully you have constructed your aëroplane, you will find the planes have a tendency to sag and become wrinkled. These braces give you the opportunity to pull them taut and hold them in this position. This is commonly called "tuning up" the aëroplane. It will be found convenient to fasten small rings to the ends of the braces whenever they may be slipped over the ends of the frame to save the trouble of winding. The more perfectly your aëroplane is tuned up, the greater will be its speed and distance qualities.

An excellent monoplane for the beginner is shown in drawing. (Plate C.) It is very simple and easily adjusted, and when well tuned up will fly upward of two hundred feet. The two planes are built separately in the proportion indicated. The frame consists of a central

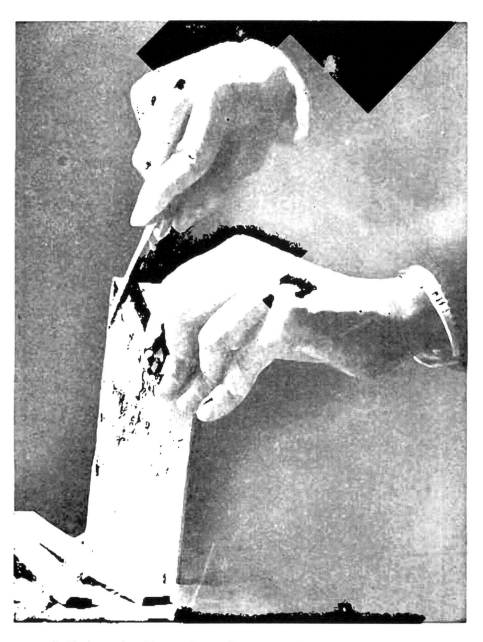

Splitting the Cigar Box Cover to Build the Propeller.

stick supported by triangular skids. An ordinary hat-pin run through the supports near the ground serves as an axle for wooden disks or wheels. The front skids are made somewhat higher to give the front planes the proper angle of elevation.

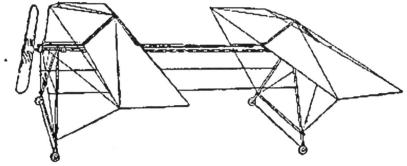

THE DIAGRAM OF A MONOPLANE.

Planes measure 20 inches by 8 inches. The motor base is 36 inches in length.

PLATE C.

The bracing of the planes is simple but effective, and should be copied carefully, particularly the double bracing in the rear, using ordinary wire for the purpose. A double support is used for the axle of the propeller, an excellent idea, which keeps the shaft rigidly in place. It is formed by fastening two blocks drilled to hold the axle to the bottom of the main frame. The planes are held taut by wires running from the corners to a post at the middle of the plane. The front plane is hinged at its rear edge, and may be tilted by pulling back a piece of whalebone fastened at its center, which is tacked to the top of the frame. The rudder turns on a triangular frame attached to the top of the rear plane. A string passes through the rear end of the rudder to the rear edge of the plane, forming a triangle, which makes it possible to adjust the rudder-plane and fix it rigidly in position.

After you have built one or two models you will find yourself confronted by a bewildering number of schemes for constructing new forms. It will be found a very simple matter to use stiff wire for many parts of your model instead of wood or reed. In building rounded planes the wire will be a convenience. The wire may be attached to the wooden frame by embedding it in the wood and binding it fast. And, by the way, you can get a surprising effect by painting your wooden frame with silver paint, as the Wrights do. To all appearance you will have an aluminium frame.

An aëroplane to be considered shipshape must be even more perfect in every detail than the finest racing yacht. Go over your model, scrutinize every detail; if after taking every precaution, your planes do not fit like the sails of a racing yacht, cover them with a thin solution of paraffin. On hardening, this will hold the material perfectly smooth, so that the planes will offer a perfect lifting surface.

The amateur aëronaut must be prepared for disappointments. An aëroplane is one of the crankiest crafts in the world to manage. It may twist and turn, plunge in and out, up and down, apparently without the least excuse. There is always, however, a good reason somewhere for its behavior. As you learn its ways, which, after all, are very simple, the flights will be longer, swiftier, and steadier. There is no toy in the world which so quickly repays one for patience and perseverance.

CHAPTER V

A GREAT many experiments have been made to find whether the flat or curved wings give the best support, and how sharply the curve should be drawn. The wings of birds are curved slightly upward, and in the end, after all the experiments, it has been found that this curve is just the right one. All forms of aëroplanes will fly more swiftly and steadily if the planes be slightly bowed or flexed. After you have built your aëroplane with flat wings it will repay you to replace them with flexed planes, and you will find that the experience in building models will make this construction very simple.

The lighter and more flexible materials, such as bamboo or cane, are best for the curved planes. After you have decided upon the dimensions of the wings cut the pieces for the ends slightly longer than the width of your planes. These pieces may then be bent by steaming them over a kettle of boiling water and bending to the desired curve. When dry they will hold their shape remarkably well. Another plan is to use a flexible strip and pull the ends together by a strong thread or wire until the wood is bowed to just the right curve. A corset steel or whalebone may readily be curved in the same way. It is a common mistake to curve the plane too sharply, when the resistance offered to the air will be greater than that with the flat plane.

A plane two or three feet in width cannot be held in shape merely by curving the end pieces. A series of ribs must be added at equal distances, each having, of course, exactly the same upward curve. The ribs may be fastened to the sides of the planes with small brads or simply with glue or wire. The covering should then be drawn down. A very smooth covering may be made of rice-paper. Cut the sheets the proper size and lay them for a few minutes between moistened cloths. Now stretch the paper carefully over the frame and glue in position. When dry the paper will contract and leave a smooth, taut surface like the head of a drum.

Much depends upon the curve of the plane. A wing whose curve is not a perfect arc of a circle, but which is rounded just back of the front edge and flattened at the rear, will be found to offer the least resistance to the air. The best plan is to study the curves in the aëroplanes or models and imitate them. Different models require different planes. It is a problem which each young aëronaut must work out for himself.

The question of rudders or guiding planes is very important. It is too much to expect of even the best model that it will fly in an unswerving line. Any simple vertical plane which may be turned from side to side and held in position will act as a rudder. There is great difference of opinion as to the proper size and position

A Model Aëroplane Built from the Drawing (Plate C, Chap. IV).

of these guiding surfaces. It is argued by some aviators that the rudder should be placed above the plane, where the air is undisturbed, while others believe that the partial vacuum created above the wings in flight makes the propeller ineffective. Still others argue that a rudder placed back of the planes affords a leverage, and is therefore more effective. Try a rudder in each position. It is impossible to lay down a law for all models.

The larger models should be equipped with twin propellers. In building these the greatest care should be taken to have them exactly the same size, weight, and pitch. Twin propellers should, as a rule, be placed at the front of the machine, that is, they should pull and not push the planes. If by any accident the motor of one should fail, the second propeller will continue to keep the aëroplane afloat and break its fall on descending. With the propellers at the stern of the little airship, the failure of one would cause the plane to pitch downward, and the remaining propeller would drive it down to possible disaster.

In winding up the two motors, care should be taken to give both the same number of turns. The aëroplane may be launched by holding a propeller in either hand and releasing simultaneously. The double motòr insures a steadier as well as a longer flight. Always turn the propellers in opposite directions. In flying they must spin around either toward each other or away from each other. If they turn the same way they will give the model a torque which no rudder could possibly overcome.

The efficiency of your motor depends more upon its length than its diameter. In constructing the motor-base, especially for the larger models, arrange to have the strands of rubber bands extend the entire length of your aëroplane, and if necessary, project well forward of the front plane. Such a motor in unwinding will exert a more sustained force. The shorter strands of greater diameter will unwind much more quickly and give very short flights.

With a little experience you will soon learn to gauge your motor to the needs of your air-ship. It is, of course, absolutely necessary that the force exerted by the motor should be sufficient to keep your aëroplane in rapid motion, but it is easy to make it too powerful. If it were possible to attach a "governor" to your motor, this would not matter so much. But since this is practically out of the question, the motor itself must be very nicely proportioned to the demand made upon it. You will soon be able to judge between the steady whir of a good motor, and the buzz of a propeller which races. There is a distinct note for each.

The motor is, at present, the great problem of the model aëroplane. The rubber bands are, at best, only a make-shift. It is practically out of the question to get a flight of more than fifteen seconds in this way, so that the distance is limited to a little more than two hundred feet. It is doubtless only a question of time before a much more efficient form of motor will be invented. Very probably, some amateur aviator will be the first to apply a new means of propulsion, which would be an important achievement indeed.

The simplest form of motor after the rubber bands would seem to be some form of metal spring which could be wound up. Long before the days of automobiles, as we now know them, wagons were built with motors of springs, and some surprising runs were obtained. The spring lends itself to many forms of construction, and is not expensive. It will be necessary to control its action in some way, however, to prevent it from racing and running down in almost no time, like the too heavy rubber motors. It might be found interesting to experiment with the spring to be found in the ordinary roller-shade. The weight of these springs is not too great to be carried by a good aëroplane model, which, of course, is a great factor in their favor.

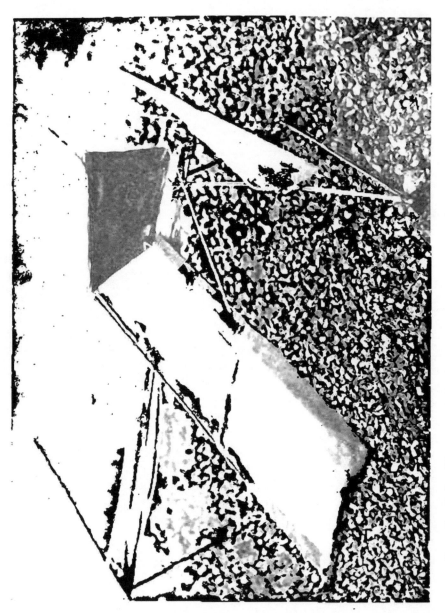

Detail of Rudder and Propeller of Model Built from Drawing (Plate C).

FINE POINTS OF CONSTRUCTION

A number of experiments have been made in France to equip aëroplane models with compressed-air motors. The compressed air is carried in a hollow tube in much the same position as the rubber bands. Many believe that the motor problem, for the toy aëroplane will be solved in this way. A number of interesting models have also been equipped with clock-work motors. A small movement, such as may be borrowed from some mechanical toys, will run for a minute or more. What glorious flights would be possible if our models could be kept aloft — say five times as long as at present. When you feel that you thoroughly understand your model, borrow the clock work from some old toy and make the experiment. It is possible to buy motors for model aëroplanes. The smallest of these develops one half horsepower, weighs seven pounds and will run for fifteen minutes.

The best covering for the wings still remains largely an open question. Although your model will make successful flights with almost any kind of covering, you will find that its stability will be increased and the flight lengthened by a little attention to this detail. According to the Wright Brothers, the most successful covering is the one which offers the greatest resistance to the air. The pressure of the air upward under the planes tends to force its way through the meshes of even the finest cloth. The addition of a coat of varnish will prevent this leakage. A light parchment will also be found effective. It will be well to experiment with a variety of coverings.

A very light, serviceable frame may be made for your motor-base by using hollow shafts or sticks. Procure a very thin, light wood, such as is used for veneering, and after cutting it carefully into strips, glue them together to form a hollow shaft about an inch square. Although the shell may be only one sixteenth of an inch thick, the frame will be found strong enough for all practical purposes. A hollow frame of this kind will save several ounces of weight.

The builder of aëroplane models will find a good friend in aluminium. It is strong enough for all purposes of the model air-ship and, even when used freely, adds almost nothing to the weight. The metal costs ninety cents a pound, but it is so light that, at this rate, it will be found a very cheap material. Comparatively thick pieces may be used for braces or for angles, thus making the frame absolutely rigid, while adding but a fraction of an ounce to the weight. The metal, being comparatively soft, is easily worked, and simple castings may be made at little expense.

Many builders of aëroplanes waste time and ingenuity quite unnecessarily in constructing sets of wheels for carrying their models. The time would be better employed in looking to your planes. The amount of friction saved by attaching wheels, even good ones, to your model, is after all very trifling. Should the wheels jam or stick, which is likely to be the case with such small models, they are worse than skids, and besides, add appreciably to the weight. A light skid is better than a clumsy wheel. If your model fails to rise from the ground, the fault is not at all likely to be in the skids, but in the thrust or lifting-surface.

An excellent plan for guiding the flights is to add square frames of soft lead wire to the front or cutting-edge of your front planes. Bend a piece of wire to form three sides of a square, each two or three inches long, and fasten the loose ends to the plane. By bending these up or down, the center of gravity may be altered at a touch. If your model goes askew, you may bend one of these up and the other down, until you get the desired balance.

In actual practice, the soaring- or floating-planes seem to add greater stability to the model and effect to a marked degree the length of the flight. It is difficult to tell exactly why. The planes in passing may create an eddy in the air, a following wave, as it were, which tends to retard the flight, while the floating-plane smoothes this out. In any event, here is an experiment well worth trying.

CHAPTER VI

SIMPLE MONOPLANE MODELS

OF the variety of aëroplanes, there seems to be no end. Nature offers a bewildering variety of models in the innumerable birds and insects, which may be accepted as successful monoplanes. These, in turn, may be copied and modified indefinitely. The science of aviation is still so young that there is ample opportunity for invention and discovery for all, and every new trial adds something to our information, and carries the science a step nearer perfection.

It will be found an excellent plan to build, once and for all, a strong well proportioned motor base, and mount a powerful motor and well modeled propeller. A variety of planes may then be tested out by attaching them to this. The motor base will answer for practically all monoplane forms and many biplane models as well. Such a frame should be about three feet in length and carry one or better two motors, placed side by side.

There is as much danger in providing too much lifting-surface in your aëroplane as too little. This fault is well illustrated in an exceedingly clever French model (Plate I). Although the model is well constructed, and appears ship-shape at first glance, it nevertheless has far too much surface and will not fly well. If the depth of the wings were reduced fully one half, it would have a much better chance.

The best lifting-planes are those which present a broad front or entering edge, but with comparatively little depth. The successful flying-machines, whether monoplanes or biplanes, use these very wide but shallow planes forward. The theory is of course that the air is caught for an instant beneath the plane and before it has a chance to slip off the sides, the wing has caught its very slight supporting power and moved on to new and undisturbed air.

With this rule in mind examine the model's front plane once more. It will be seen that, as the air is caught under this broad surface, it will try to escape in all directions and set up currents of air. Instantly the broad plane loses its balance and tilts to one side or the other. No weighting of the plane can overcome this. If the plane were forced through the air at a very high speed a steady flight might be possible, but it is useless to try to overcome this tendency to tip and wabble.

The planes again are badly designed. A perfectly straight front or entering edge gives the best results. A certain stability is gained by curving the front plane slightly, this will be discussed later, but there is no excuse for the semicircle described in this case. Every inch of surface cut away from the front edge of the plane directly reduces its lifting power. The arrow like form of the rear plane does not matter because this is a stability plane,

PLATE I.

A Clever Folding Model. The Wings Are Broader than Need Be.

not a lifting plane. In this case the rear plane is twice the size it should be.

The propeller of this model is much too small, even if the size of the planes was correct. It is well placed however at the front of the model where it may turn in undisturbed air. The passage of these large planes, or any planes for that matter, is likely to cut up the air just as a ship churns the water into a wake behind it and the propeller does not work effectively in these eddies. The motor seems powerful and well braced, although it might be made even longer by carrying it to the extreme rear.

Several very useful ideas may be borrowed from the construction of the frame of this model. It is made entirely of metal, so jointed that it may be folded up into very compact form like an umbrella. The amateur model builder should not attempt anything so complicated, but an old umbrella frame may be used with good results in building a rigid frame. Use the steel rod of the umbrella as a backbone, and cut away the ribs you do not need. The others may be bent into various shapes to form the front or sides of the planes, the skids or braces. Such a construction is light and perfectly rigid.

A very effective monoplane may be made by curving the front and rear edges of the forward plane, while keeping the rear or stability plane rectangular in shape (Plate 2). The curve of this model may be imitated to advantage, as well as the general proportions. Such a plane is less likely to be deflected by air currents than a straight entering-edge and insures longer and steadier flights. Should you be troubled by your model twisting from side to side in flight try curving the front edge of the forward plane.

This model is one of the easiest to make and is an excellent one for beginners. Build the two planes separately making the larger one about thirty inches in width and ten inches in depth, and the second one fifteen inches in width and ten inches in depth. The curved sticks may be worked up by using bamboo or dowel sticks, soaking them in water and fastening them in a bowed position while damp and leaving them to dry. It may be found a good plan to use a heavier stick for the rear edge of the plane to gain stability.

A single stick about one half an inch in diameter may be used for the backbone. It will be found an excellent plan to attach the planes lightly to the main frame so that they may be adjusted before fixing them finally in position. Place them in the position shown in the accompanying photograph, and move them up and down until the flights are all that you expect, when they may be fastened for good and all. The bracing of this model is excellent and may be safely imitated. It enables one to tune up either plane and fix them rigidly in position. The propeller is very properly placed forward although it appears to be rather small. It is unnecessary to bother with any vertical rudder for this model since the curve of the front plane insures a reasonably straight flight.

MODEL AEROPLANES

A popular French model which may be easily imitated consists of curved planes both front and rear (Plate 3). The curve of the planes is too complicated to be carried out in wood, but may be readily formed by bending a stiff wire to the desired shape. The front plane should be about twelve inches in width and four inches in depth. The rear should be about half this size and of the same form. The planes may be readily mounted on a small dowel stick. A small propeller and a motor a foot in length will answer. A small semi-circular fin should be set below the rear plane to act as rudder. First cover the frames with a stiff paper and after you have succeeded in adjusting it, this may be replaced by cloth. The model will not fly far, or very steadily, but it is interesting to practice with. The balance of the model is open to criticism; for the center of gravity appears to be too far forward.

The simplest of all models to build, and not the least interesting, is the small paper

A Model Aëroplane Worth Imitating.

monoplane (Plate 4). The planes which are slightly curved are formed of a stiff card which will hold its shape when bent into position. These may be attached to the main stick by inserting an edge into a groove in the stick and glueing in place. It is not well to construct these more than six inches in width over all.

One of the simplest monoplanes to construct is formed of a broad rectangular forward plane with a fan-shaped stability-plane at the rear (Plate 5). This is a French model which is said to have flown long distances; that is to say, 300 feet or more. It has several very interesting features. In the first place the combined area of its planes is doubtless greater than that of any other model here described. The vertical rudder which looks very ship-shape and effective is very easy to build and the frame illustrates several new principles.

The frame or motor-base may be made of heavy dowel sticks or light lath as indicated in the photograph. It will be found simpler to avoid tapering the frame at the rear by merely constructing a stout rectangular base with a length two and one half times its width. The forward plane is slightly bowed or flexed. It will be found a good plan to construct the frame for the base and then bow a light strip at either end against the edge. By fastening the covering to these curved strips a smooth curved surface may be obtained.

The rear stability-plane may be stretched over a fan-shaped frame of strips or lath which is in turn fastened to the motor-base. Another plan is to attach the front and rear edges of the plane, the rear one being slightly longer, and stretch the covering over these leaving the sides free as in the photograph of the accompanying model. The vertical rudder is very simple, consisting of a piece of dowel stick sunk in the rear frame to which a rectangular piece of cloth is attached the front corner being pulled taut.

The spread of the planes appears to be considerably greater than needs be. Since the front plane is flexed it may be reduced one third or even one half in depth without reducing its lifting quality; although in this case it should be placed nearer the stability plane. This reduction would, of course, make an important saving in the weight of the craft. So large a model calls for two propellers which will prove more effective at the front rather than the rear of the machine. It might be well to carry the motors further back than has been done in this model thus gaining additional power.

Since the model is expected to rise unaided from the ground the question of the skids is very important. The design followed in the model is excellent. The front of the frame is supported by legs consisting of inverted triangles built of dowel sticks attached to the frame. The axle connecting the two runs on small wheels, such as may be borrowed from a toy automobile. The rear of the frame rests on a simple skid made of curved reed. These supports place the model at an angle which should enable it to rise easily without loss of power. There is a great deal of satisfaction in working on so large a model, the parts may be made stronger and there is less likelihood of its getting out of order.

Now turn from these broad planes to the rather slight model (Plate 6), and the faults of its proportion are at once obvious. The front plane is much too far back for stability. Such a model will glide fairly well, and, if the motor be powerful it will rise quickly, but a steady horizontal flight is out of the question. The size of the planes seems perilously small, and yet if they be well shaped and spaced they will prove large enough. This is just the sort of model a beginner is likely to make, and therefore serves a very useful purpose in pointing a lesson.

It is not without its good points. The front plane has been carefully flexed and attached to the motor frame at a good angle. An interesting experiment has also been made in carrying the edges of the

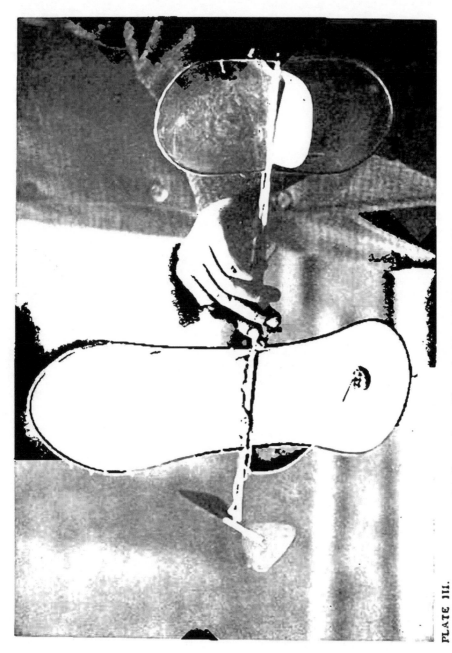

PLATE III. An Ingenious French Model Made of Umbrella Wire.

front plane a trifle behind the rear edge, thus making for stability. The vertical rudder above the rear stability-plane is well placed, although it appears rather small. The skids upon which the model rests and the proportion of the front to the rear elevation are excellent. It is a first rate plan in building such a model to attach the front plane temporarily to the motor-base, and move it back and forth in the trial flights until the best spacing has been found.

CHAPTER VII

ELABORATING THE MONOPLANE

IT is surprising to find how far the pure monoplane form has been developed by the builders of model aëroplanes. It is no exaggeration to say that they have carried some principles of construction even further than the builders of the large man-carrying monoplanes. Since a model is so easily built, and costs so little, it is of course possible to experiment with all sorts of new forms. A great many of these will doubtless prove to be all wrong, but some are certain to be valuable discoveries. In future years, when the aëroplane has been perfected and perhaps plays an important part in commerce, sport and warfare it will probably be possible to trace back many of its improvements to the model aëroplanes designed, built and flown by American boys of to-day.

A beautiful model of a pure monoplane form carefully elaborated is shown in Plate 7. In this case increased stability is obtained by throwing out additional planes both to the front and rear. It may appear at first glance that these stability-planes are very small compared with the broad soaring-plane, but they have not proved so in flight. It will be remembered that the elevating-plane of the Wright machine is very small compared with the spread of the main wings. There is besides a great advantage in placing the stability plane well forward since it makes it possible to build an unusually long motor-base and install longer and more powerful motors.

The main plane is one of the best examples of construction work to be found among all these models. It is well proportioned and the curve has been skilfully drawn. The plane is made unusually rigid by a series of supports or braces run both

horizontally and vertically. Such a plane
calls for considerable time and patience,
but it will well repay the builder by the
long and steady flights it insures for the
model. In adding ribs to a large plane of
this kind a convenient material may be
prepared by splitting up thin wooden
plates or dishes, such as you buy at the
grocers for a penny. The strips obtained
in this way may be easily glued or tied to
the edge of the plane and shaped as desired.

A long, straight flight is insured for this
model by equipping it with three vertical
rudders or guiding-planes. The first rudder is well placed above the front plane.
The second performs a good service beneath the main plane, while the third is
carried unusually far back behind the propellers. The problem whether a rudder
is more effective above or below the planes
is very ingeniously solved in this case by
placing them in both positions. An interesting principle is involved in placing
the rear rudder. By fixing it far behind

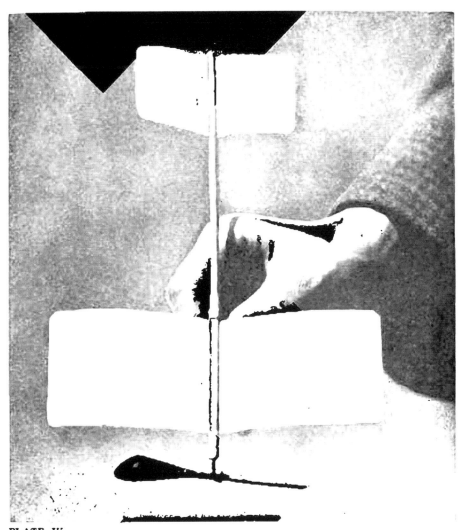

PLATE IV.
One of the Simplest of Aëroplanes to Construct.

the center of gravity of the model a considerable leverage is obtained, and a small, light rudder becomes more effective in this position than a much larger plane placed forward. These rudders are built so that they may be easily turned from side to side and fixed rigidly at any angle.

Still another interesting feature of this model is the design of the skids. The model is supported at an angle which enables it to rise easily. These skids are besides arranged with shock-absorbers, simply constructed with elastic bands, which enable them to take up the shock on landing and thus protects the machine. This is an interesting field of experiment and a little care in building these skids will save many a smash-up.

It cannot be too often stated, that the supporting power of the planes depends far more upon their shape than their size. A remarkably effective model may be made with planes, which are little more than blades (Plate 8). The planes, in this case, are made of white wood, slightly curved. The front or entering edge is very sharp, while, at the rear, a thin strip of shellaced silk is glued, thus forming a good soaring blade. The front plane is a counterpart of the first, except that it is smaller. The only stability plane is a thin, knife-like strip placed vertically just before the rear plane. The model is mounted on skids. It is driven by a small propeller placed far back of the center of gravity. It is probably the easiest as it is the smallest of all models to construct, and will fly for more than three hundred feet.

In building this model it will be found a good plan to bend the strips of wood for the planes by steaming them over a kettle. Allow the steam to play on the under or concave side of the plane. When dry the plane will retain its shape. The front or entering edge should be trimmed away to a sharp line and sand-papered perfectly smooth. The front corners of the planes should be slightly rounded while the rear edges are kept straight. The forward plane should be tilted slightly upward to enable it to rise, but at an angle of less than thirty degrees. The secret of the remarkable flights of this model probably lies in the smoothness of its planes and the absence of irregular parts which offer a resistance to the air.

An interesting field of experiment, as yet almost untouched, lies in the triangular, or narrow-prowed forms of aëroplanes (Plate 9). The theory of this model is, that a triangle entering the air end-wise, will meet with less resistance than when presenting a broad, entering edge. The model is, frankly, an experiment, although it has been found to have unexpected stability, and flies well. Its central planes, joined at right angles, is supported by two, lateral, stability-planes, radiating backward from the front of the model. The aëroplane is drawn, not pushed, through the air, by double propellers, and is steered by an angular guiding-plane at the rear. The planes are mounted upon a triangular frame, which runs on wheels, two being set forward and one aft. The planes, taking advantage of the dihedral angle, seem to rest upon the air, which makes for stability. In actual practice, however, the planes in this particular model have been found to be too narrow. The question naturally arises as to the effect of reversing this model and turning the dihedral angle of the central plane, into a tent effect. As a matter of actual experience, the model flies almost equally well upside down.

In many of the early attempts to build aëroplanes the wings or planes were tilted sharply upward from the center thus forming what is known as a dihedral angle. This form served to lower the center of gravity and, it was thought, made for stability. The Wright Brothers found that this plan, although it lowered the center of gravity, caused it to move from side to side like a pendulum, and therefore abandoned it in favor of the flat curved wing which have been so generally imitated. Now this model returns to the old principle of the dihedral model, but treats

PLATE V.
Too Large for Beginners, but Will Make Long Flights.

it in a new way. By building the model with three planes, each with the dihedral angle, the center of gravity has been lowered and, at the same time, the oscillation has been greatly reduced.

The narrow-prowed form of this model is also very interesting and its principle may well be copied. All of the successful monoplanes aloft to-day, the Bleriot, Santos Dumont, Antoinette and others are driven with their larger or soaring planes forward and their smaller stability-planes in the rear. The day may come when these machines will be reversed. The model before us may point the way to a great improvement in the building of air-craft. It is an important principle for the builder of model aëroplanes to bear in mind.

In the present state of model aëroplane building, the longest flights are made with an adaptation of the monoplane forms. An excellent model is shown in Plate 10. The dihedral, or V shape of the planes gives them greater supporting power than others in the horizontal position. The stability plane beneath is particularly recommended, since it utilizes the frame already in position and does not add to the weight of the model. The rear of this plane, which is hinged, is easily adjusted.

The planes of this model are especially interesting. They are made of silk, laid over frames of dowel sticks, and each pair is held tightly together by the simple device of connecting them with elastic bands, attached to clasps. The wires running to the corners of the planes, are fastened to small brass rings which may be slipped over the sticks or posts in the center of the frame, which makes them very simple to adjust. It will be noticed that the rear part of each plane swings freely, and is kept in place only by corset steels, used as ribs, which are sewn into the cloth. These floating or soaring blades, as they are sometimes called, insure longer flights.

With such a model there is little danger of building a too powerful motor. By increasing the size of the wings, and careful weighting, a surprising amount of power may be applied to such a model without rendering it unstable. This is of course a great advantage in such a model, since it lends itself to longer flights and the installation of comparatively heavy motors. When you find yourself with a model of this design in good working order, experiment by binding the wings or planes at the middle to form an arched surface like the wings of a sea gull. The flying radius of some of these models has been increased fully fifty per cent by this simple expedient.

An interesting modification of this form (Plate 11) is provided with rigid wings, and is driven by a single propeller. The very simple but effective method of bracing the wings, may be studied to advantage. The skids are well designed. In still another type of this general monoplane form (Plate 12) the propeller is placed in front of the planes, and the rubber motor runs below the main bar. The wheels supporting this model are particularly well made.

A very serviceable, little monoplane form may be made by making the rear upper plane adjustable (Plates 13-14). The front plane is V-shaped and is unusually stable for so light a model. By tilting the rear plane up or down, a good level flight may be obtained. The frame, in this case, is made of wire. The propeller is placed well behind the rear plane, thus bringing the center of gravity well forward to balance the angle of the rear plane. The blades of the propeller are made of twisted wood, which is not to be recommended, since it is likely to lose its shape.

In Plates 15-16 we have a well thought out little monoplane, which well repays study. The propeller is set forward of the lifting plane which is the larger of the wings. The rear plane may be tilted up or down. The rudder, which is also adjustable, is set below it. The arrangement of skids is excellent, enabling it to rise from the ground with little loss of

Model shown in Plate V.   Ready for a Flight.

friction. The method of flexing the front plane may well be imitated.

A good working idea of the aëroplane is clearly shown by the builder of the biplane with triangular wings (Plate 17). His model is not successful and will not fly, yet it embodies several good features. The biplane form of the lifting plane is excellent in itself as we have seen in earlier models. The spacing of the two planes is good, and the bracing of the model throughout is well planned. The triangle does not make a good soaring plane even when its broad side is made the entering edge. The triangle serves well enough however for the rear stability plane. The chief fault of the model is that it is much too large. The motor although well proportioned is much too weak to propel so large a frame.

An interesting variation from the common type of aëroplane is made by varying the angle of the sides of the planes (Fig. 18). Here is a well constructed model, and, with a single exception, fairly well proportioned. The mistake, and it is likely to prove a serious one, is in the size of the vertical rudders. They are well placed above the main plane, but their size is likely to defeat the purpose for which they were designed and knock the model off its course rather than keep it steady. It is a question again if one of these rudders would not serve the purpose better than two and thus minimize weight and resistance.

The best point of this model is the ingenious method of enlarging the surface of the planes without increasing the size of the planes or adding to their weight. This is done by cutting the covering of the planes at an angle and keeping the entire surface taut by bracing. It is of course very important that the cloth should be held tight without wrinkling. The plan of having the wings taper slightly outward is good. Such a model combines more lifting surface with less weight than any other model of this general group.

CHAPTER VIII

EVERY one knows, of course, that the box-kite flies better than a plane surface, and many believe that the box or cellular type of aëroplane has a similar advantage over the monoplane. The enclosed end keeps the air from slipping off the edges of the plane, and makes for stability. There is all the difference in the world, or rather in the air, between an actual flight and the movement of a model aëroplane. The aviator, by flexing his planes, and adjusting his rudders fore and aft, may balance his craft to suit the air currents. In the model aëroplane, the adjustment must be made before starting once and for all. Several interesting principles are involved in the cellular or box form of aëroplanes which will well repay study (Plates 19-20).

In disturbed air, which is of course the usual condition of the atmosphere, the cellular model is likely to be deflected, and since the elevating plane or planes cannot be adjusted, it will soon fall off its course. Such models are easy to construct, and any one who has built a monoplane will have little difficulty with them. No attempt is made to flex the planes. The cellular type must be equipped with a lifting-plane forward, which may be easily adjusted to any angle, and held in position. It is indispensable that you have two propellers placed aft behind the main plane. The model may be made much more effective by adding a third stability-plane or rudder at the rear. It may be either vertical or horizontal and should be easily adjusted. The models illustrated, herewith, are very simple forms and clearly indicate the necessary frame work. It will be found that these models require considerable ballast, skilfully distributed.

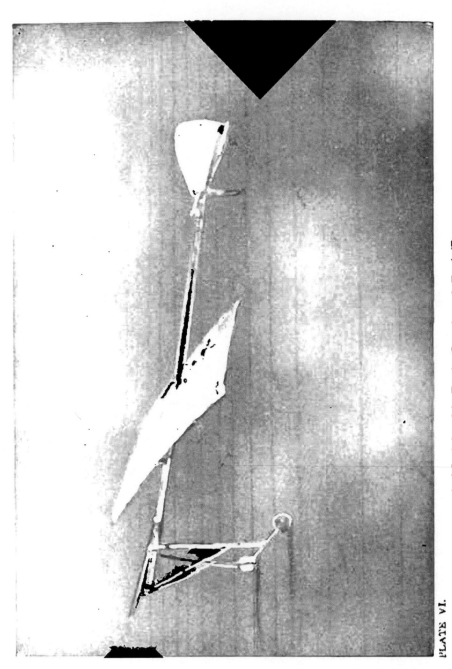

A Model with Both Good and Bad Features.

PLATE VI.

BUILDING A BIPLANE

In building these cellular forms select some light lath for the frame rather than dowel sticks. It will be necessary to join many of these together at right angles, and the curved stick will be found difficult to work. For each box cut four sticks the desired width, and eight sticks the depth of your plane. The box should be almost exactly square so that all these shorter sticks should be the same length. Now build your box by nailing and glueing these sticks together, taking great pains to have it symmetrical. Should a single one of these sticks be too long or too short it will throw the entire frame out of plumb and make it next to impossible to get a straight flight.

In most of these models the front or rear stability-planes are made exactly like the larger frame only much smaller. When the frames are completed and thoroughly dry and smooth, stretch the cloth covering tightly over them by drawing it length-wise, all the way around. By using a single piece of cloth it will be found easier to pull it together and hold it tight and smooth. It will be found a good plan to touch the outer edges of the frame you are covering with glue just before covering. When the glue dries the cloth will thus be held firmly in position. The cloth may be fastened to the outer edges by glueing or sewing.

A simple but effective plan for mounting the stability-planes is suggested by the models here illustrated. The frame of the motor-base may be made the width of the smaller frame and fastened between the two sticks. It should be left free so that it may be tilted up or down and fixed in any position. If the rear stability-plane is to serve as rudder it should of course be mounted vertically so that it may be turned to right or left. Be sure to make your frame sufficiently strong and rigid. A light frame which will vibrate when the motor turns or is shaken by the wind will be found very troublesome indeed.

The cylindrical forms of planes (Plate 21) carries the foregoing principles a step further. A surprising degree of stability is obtained by thus enclosing the air, and by throwing out several lateral stability-planes fore and aft. The models may be constructed of heavy wire, ordinary umbrella wire will answer the purpose, and may be readily bent. The planes in the accompanying model are merely suggestive. The broad planes placed forward, well above the diameter, promise well, but the rear wings appear unstable and small for the other surface. The forward or lifting-plane is again, much too narrow. The cylindrical form is equipped with a double propeller, one before and the other in the rear, both mounted on a bar, which forms the exact axis of the cylinder. This adjustment will give you a very pleasant surprise. The vibration and torque of the two propellers seem to equalize one another, and the thrust is much more steady than in the case of a single screw. The thrust is not only double, in this way, but the gain for stability is surprising. The model should be mounted on skids to assist it in rising, and to take up the force of the impact on landing.

The double propeller, mounted on the same shaft, may be used successfully in many models. A very simple monoplane form (Plate 22) may be equipped in this way. If two or more planes be mounted between the propellers, an astonishing soaring quality may be had. It is an excellent plan to fasten the planes to the frame at first by rubber bands, so that they may be pushed up or down readily, and adjusted and weighted to suit the conditions.

There is danger in this form, however, that the plane will turn completely over in its flight, although this will have little effect upon the thrust or direction. The model is exceedingly simple to make. The propellers should not be too large, not more than twice the diameter of the planes at most. The two propellers must, of course, be turned in opposite directions, to correct the twisting tendency.

Should you construct a motor-base of

PLATE VII.

A Good Example of Careful Designing and Workmanship.

this kind with propellers at either end it will be found interesting to experiment by attaching planes of different shapes and sizes. It requires very little surface to keep such a monoplane afloat. Instead of the circular and elliptical plane placed lengthwise, as in the accompanying model, try the effect of larger circles and broader ellipses, placing the latter sideways. This may be varied by using small rectangular planes with the corners rounded off. Sooner or later you will hit upon a shape of plane and a spacing which will give you good, steady flights of surprising length.

It has been suggested that a good motor-base be built with double propellers and the various forms of planes tested out upon it. Let us carry this idea further and, now that we have had some experience in building aëroplane models, construct a quadruple motor-base; that is a motor-base with four strands of rubber bands and four propellers, two forward and two aft. The four would of course have to be very nicely balanced. The two sets of propellers if carefully set up would tend to correct one another, as we have seen in the cylindrical and other double propellers thus giving a very steady flight. The increased speed of such a motor would carry any good model at a much higher rate of speed than any of the present forms.

There is a very simple rule to be remembered in building all biplanes, regarding the spacing of the planes. The distance between the super-imposed planes should always be equal to the width of the planes themselves. A beautiful model (Plate 23) is here reproduced, to show how not to space your planes. In all other respects the model is excellent. The planes themselves are beautifully constructed and scientifically curved. It is interesting to note, in this case, that the front and rear sets of planes would be much too far apart were they flat surfaces, but being flexed as they are, their supporting power is greatly increased. By placing them so far apart, a longer and more powerful motor may be used. The rudders, both fore and aft, are adjustable, and appear very effective and shipshape.

The method of tuning up the planes in this model is especially to be recommended. From a post, placed at the center of the planes, wires are run to the corners which holds the frame perfectly taut. For the main frame, or backbone, a metal tube has been used which greatly adds to the appearance of the model. This aluminium tubing may be bought cheaply and will serve admirably for this purpose.

The most popular of all models, among amateur aëronauts in America, at least, is the Wright machine (Plates 24-25). The opinion is ventured that this is due more to the attractiveness of its lines and the pride we all take in its wonderful achievements, than to its actual flying ability as a model. The most perfect of these models will rarely fly more than a hundred feet. They will be found exceedingly difficult to weight and adjust so that they will maintain their course in a disturbed air current.

MODEL AEROPLANES

The planes of these models are usually made separate from the motor base. The shafts of the propellers, with the rubber motors and skids, are built up in a single piece. This plan has the advantage of making the planes adjustable so that they may move backward or forward as desired. The model leaves the ground from a base, much the same as the rail used by the large Wright machines. Some models are even started by the propulsion of a rubber band attached to the frame, which is pulled back and released, like the old-fashioned sling shot.

PLATE XVIII.

A Good Model Excepting that its Vertical Rudders Are Too Large.

CHAPTER IX

ALTHOUGH the regular biplane form is exceedingly difficult to manage in small models, there is great advantage in combining it with the monoplane forms (Plate 26). The biplane makes an excellent lifting plane, and when the model combines with it a broad monoplane for stability, surprisingly long flights may be made. The model here illustrated has flown 218 feet 6 inches.

Despite its size, the model is exceedingly light. It is made almost entirely of dowel sticks braced with piano wire. Still another advantage of the biplane form is the action of the supporting surface when it comes to descend. The model settles easily to the ground, in contrast to many monoplane models which come down with a dislocating shock. The skids of this model are simple and effective. In a model of this form it is obviously best to have the propellers drive rather than pull it.

An ingenious young aëronaut has reversed the above order and placed his biplane in the rear, using the monoplane for lifting (Plate 27). His model is unusually large, having a spread of four feet. The biplane is square, with lateral stability planes on either side. The elevating planes appear small in proportion, but they serve to keep the craft on an even keel. The most striking feature of this model is its extreme lightness. Although unusually large, it weighs but nine ounces. The frame, except for the braces is built of reed. The planes are covered with parchment. The model is driven by two rather small propellers. The position of the propellers will appear, at first glance, to be rather low, but it must be remembered that the extreme lightness of the model brings the center of gravity very far down.

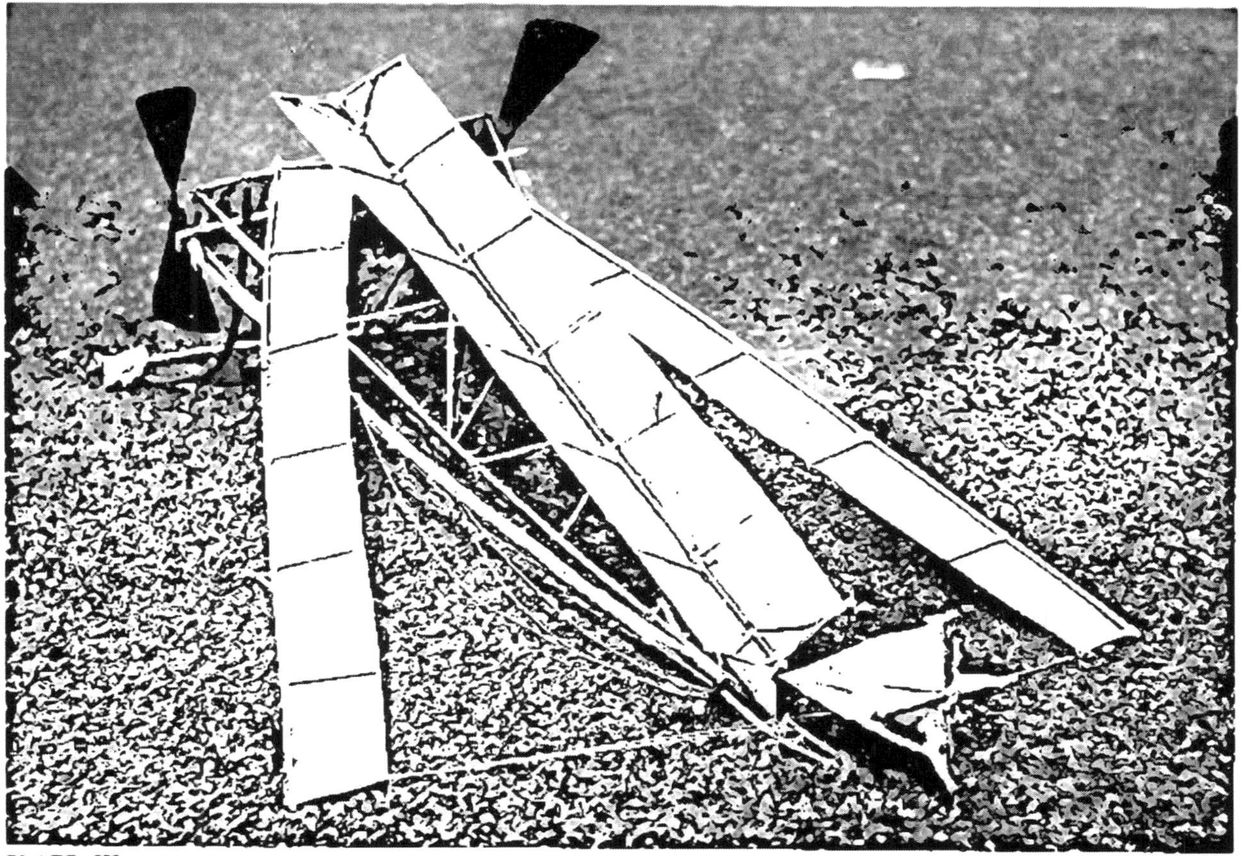

PLATE IX.

An Interesting Experiment Along New Lines.

The model has flown more than two hundred feet.

The stability of the models thus combining the monoplane and biplane forms comes as a surprise. Both the models in question rise easily from the ground, which is more than can be said of many aëroplanes big or little, and once aloft maintain a steady horizontal flight, which is still more unusual. An interesting field of experiment is suggested by these combinations. These successful experiments have been made with perfectly flat planes. Suppose now we try them out with flexed planes. If the stability thus gained may be combined with the increased soaring quality of the curved plane, we may be on the way to making some remarkable flights. In the summer of 1909 a number of boys built and flew model aëroplanes in New York, when many interesting and well constructed modes were brought out, and the longest flight was only sixty feet. Less than one year later the same boys succeeded in flying their machines for more than two hundred feet. The new models were no larger, the motors no more powerful, but the machine had become more ship shape and efficient. It is reasonable to suppose that each year will bring a similar advance.

CHAPTER X

FAULTS AND HOW TO MEND THEM

YOUR model, perhaps a beautiful one, finished in every part, may twist and tip about as soon as it is launched and quickly dart to the ground. The fault is likely to be in the propeller, being too large for the size and weight of the machine. This may be remedied by adding a weight to the front of the machine, by wiring on a nut or piece of metal. Should this fail to steady the aëroplane, the propeller must be cut down.

When your propeller is too small the machine will not rise from the ground, or, if launched in the air, will quickly flutter to earth. If the model on leaving your hand, with the propeller in full motion, fails to keep its position from the very start, the blade should be made larger.

There is no use in wasting time and patience over the machine as it is.

Many a beginner, with mistaken zeal, constructs a too powerful motor. The power in this case turns the propeller too swiftly for it to grasp the air. It merely bores a hole in the air and exerts little propelling force. An ordinary motor when wound up one hundred and fifty turns should take about ten seconds, perhaps a trifle longer, to unwind. It is a good plan to time it before chancing a flight.

Bad bracing is another frequent source of trouble. The planes should be absolutely rigid. Test your model by winding up your motor and letting it run down while keeping the aëroplane suspended, by holding it loosely in one hand. If the motor racks the machine, that is, if the little ship is all a-flutter and the planes tremble visibly, the entire frame needs tuning up. It is impossible for an aëroplane to hold its course if the planes are in the least wabbly. The braces should be taut. A loose string or wire incidentally offers as much resistance to the air as a wooden post.

The flight of your model aëroplane should be horizontal, with little or no wave-motion. Your craft at first may rise to a considerable height, say fifteen or twenty feet, then plunge downward, right itself, and again ascend, and repeat this rather violent wave-motion until it strikes the ground. To overcome this, look carefully to the angle or lift of your front plane or planes and to the weighting.

The explanation is very simple. As the aëroplane soars upward, the air is compressed beneath the planes, and this continues until the surface balances, tilts forward, and the downward flight commences. Your planes should be so inclined that the center of air-pressure comes about one third of the distance back from the front edge. The center of gravity of each plane, however, should come slightly in front of the center of pressure. After all, the best plan is to proceed by the rule of thumb, and tilt your planes little by little, and add or lessen the weight in one place or another, until the flight is horizontal and stable.

If your aëroplane does not rise from the ground, but merely slides along, the trouble is likely to be in your lifting plane. Tilt it a trifle and try again. The simplest way to do this is to make the front skids higher than those at the back. If the front skids are too high, the plane will shoot up in the air and come down within a few feet.

The most carefully constructed model is likely to go awry in the early flights. The propeller seems to exert a twist or torque, as it is called, which sends it to the right or left, or up or down, even in a perfectly undisturbed atmosphere. It is assumed that your model is symmetrical. An aëroplane not properly balanced, which is larger on one side than the other, or in which the motor is not exactly centered, cannot, of course, be expected to fly straight. However, to be on the safe side,

go all over the machine again. Measure
its planes to see that the propeller is in the
center. Hold it up in front of you right
abeam, and test with your eye if the parts
be properly balanced.

If it still flies badly askew, flex the
planes by bending the ends up or down
very slightly by tightening or loosening
the wire braces running to the corners.
At the same time add a little weight to
counteract the tipping tendency. A nut
or key may be wired on the edge which
persists in turning up. It may require
much more weight than you imagine. The
difference should begin to show at once.
Even after a model appears to work fairly
well as a glider, the addition of the motor
may so change the center of gravity that
it will " cut up " dreadfully.

It will be well to leave your planes loose
so that they may be shifted back and forth
and not fasten them till you have tried out
the motor. If you followed the plan suggested of fastening the plane to the central
frame by crossing rubber bands over it,

you can easily adjust them. If the model tends to fly upward at a sharp angle, slide the front plane forward an inch, and try another flight. There is an adjustment somewhere which will give the model the steady, horizontal flight you are after.

Some models will refuse to rise and swing around in an abrupt circle the moment the motor is turned on. This may be caused by the propeller being much too small for the motor. After looking over all the photographs of the models shown in these pages you will gain an idea of the proper proportion, and be able to tell offhand if the propeller is out of proportion. A small propeller revolving very rapidly, or racing, is likely to give the model a torque, even if it be otherwise well proportioned. Don't try to remedy this with rudder surfaces, but change your propeller, or your motor, or both.

When your aëroplane turns in long, even curves to one side or the other, look to your rudder surface. Turn it to one side or the other, just as you would in

PLATE X.

An Excellent Monoplane Capable of Long Flights.

steering a boat. It is, of course, obvious that it must be kept rigidly in position. If a slight turn of the rudder does not straighten out the flight, you probably need more guiding surface, and the rudder must be enlarged. If the model still continues to turn away from a straight line, tilting as it does so, try a little weight at the end of the plane which rises.

The commonest of all accidents to aëroplane models is the smashing up of the skids on landing. A model will frequently rise to a height of fifteen or twenty feet, and the shock of a fall from such an elevation is likely to work havoc in the under-body. There is no reason, however, why your model should not come down as lightly as a bird from the crest of the flight wave. The model, when properly proportioned, weighted, or balanced, will settle down gradually and not pitch violently. It is these quick darts to earth which cause the worst disasters.

A model should have sufficient supporting surface to break its fall when the motor runs down, at any reasonable elevation. If the model aëroplane falls all in a heap, as soon as the motor slows down, it will be well to look to this and perhaps increase the size of your planes. As a general rule, the biplanes or the models in which the double planes have been used, either for lifting or soaring planes, will settle down more gradually. The lateral planes, whatever their position, also lend valuable support when the critical time comes in the descent. Your model is not perfect until it falls easily at the end of the flight.

Under perfect condition, in absolutely undisturbed air, an aëroplane may be made to come down so lightly that no bones, even the smallest, will be broken. A gust of wind, however, may ruin all your calculations and bring the aëroplane down with a dislocating shock. The skids must be designed to meet extreme conditions, the worst that can possibly befall. It has been pointed out that these skids or supports should be high enough to give

Detail of Model Shown in Plate X.

the propeller clearance so that the propeller blades will not touch the ground. By using a light flexible cane for the purpose, and bending them under, a spring may be formed which will take up the shock of a violent landing. Some builders go further and rig up the skids with braces of rubber bands to increase this cushion effect. A variety of constructions are shown in the photographs of the various models. Your skids should enable your model to withstand any ordinary shock of landing, without breakage of any kind.

The life of your motor can be greatly increased by careful handling. The rubber strands are likely to be worn away against the hooks at either end. The wire used for the hooks should be as heavy as possible to keep it from cutting through. Be careful that the wire which comes in contact with the rubber is perfectly smooth and flawless. A little roughness or a spur on the wire will soon cut through the rubber. It is a good plan to slip a piece of rubber tubing tightly over the hook and loop the rubber bands of your motor over this cushion.

The first break in the rubber bands is likely to come near the center of the strand. A number of loose ends appear. The broken ends should be knotted neatly and the loose ends cut away. If the strands come in contact with any part of the motor base, a breaking will quickly follow, and your strands soon become covered with a fringe of loose ends. Be careful to tie up all loose ends and trim them away, since the ends in twisting serve to break other strands. Although the finer strands of rubber give the greater thrust, do not buy them too small, since they are easily broken.

The length of your motor base beyond the front plane should be carefully calculated. It is very easy, of course, to run your shaft too far forward. The center of gravity is easily shifted in this way, and your model soon becomes unmanageable. An aëroplane with this fault will not rise, but merely pitches forward under the

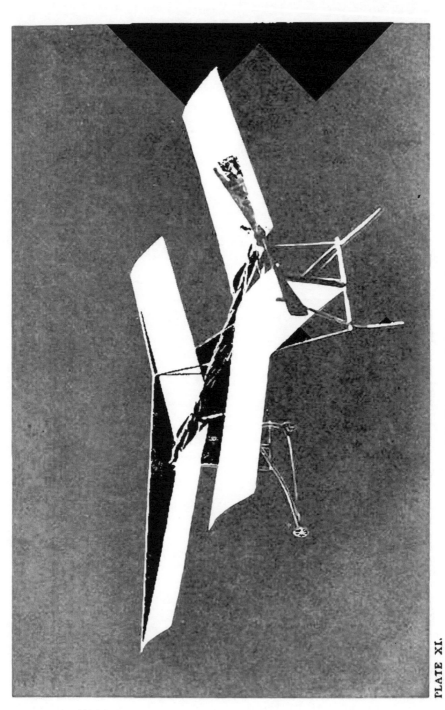

PLATE XI.

A Well Thought Out Monoplane.

thrusts of the motor. It is almost useless to attempt to balance this by weighting the machine. The front plane should be placed further forward, and if the lifting surface does not seem sufficient, cut away the front of your motor base, once for all. A too short motor base, on the other hand, will cause your model to shoot upward at a sharp angle, and waste much valuable propelling power before it rights itself and takes a regular horizontal flight.

In the model aëroplane there is only one point where friction affects the flight, namely, along the propeller shaft. One can hardly be too careful in the construction of the axle. The thrust of the rubber at best, is limited, and this power must be exerted without loss of any kind. A faulty propeller shaft will use up a surprising amount of energy. Your rubber motor should unwind to within one or two turns.

Bear in mind that one of four things is likely to be responsible for your trouble. The planes may not be properly placed on the frame, they may not be properly flexed, they are not set at the proper angle of elevation, or your motor is at fault. Watch these points, and you will soon have your machine under perfect control. In the extremely complicated models it is often difficult to locate the fault. Build your model so that these parts may be adjusted in a moment without taking apart. After you have built an aëroplane model, even a very simple one, the pictures of other aëroplanes will have a new meaning for you. Every new model you see will give you some new idea. A number of the most successful aëroplane models in the country are shown in the accompanying photographs. Study these carefully, and you will learn more from them of practical aëroplane construction than from any amount of reading.

PART II

THE HISTORY AND SCIENCE OF AVIATION

CHAPTER I

THE FIRST FLYING MACHINES

THE conquest of the air was not won by a happy accident of invention. Long before man learned to fly the science of aviation had to be created by investigation and experiment. At first with very crude attempts, a great many flying machines had to be built, and many lives sacrificed in flying them. The exact nature of the invisible air currents and the action of wings and planes, were to be learned before the delicate mechanism of the modern aëroplane was possible. Probably no other great invention has required such long and patient preparation.

In many ways the aëroplane is therefore a greater achievement than the steam engine or the steamboat. When Watt turned from watching his tea kettle to build his engine, he applied mechanical principles which had long been in actual use, and there were many experienced mechanics to help him. Robert Fulton, again, when he set up his engine, found the science of boat-building highly developed. The aviator had no such advantage. He must first of all build a craft which would keep afloat in the most unstable of mediums. A motive power had to be applied to suit these conditions, and the two must be so attuned that they would work perfectly together when the least slip would mean instant disaster. As we learn to realize these difficulties we will appreciate more than ever how marvellous a creation is the modern aëroplane.

Man has thought much about flying from the earliest times. The open air has always seemed the natural highway, and flying machines were invented hundreds of years before anyone dreamed of steam-engines or steamboats. The ancient Greeks long ago spun wonderful tales of the mythical Daedalus and Icarus and

PLATE XII.

A Good Example of Tilted Planes.

their flight to the sun and back again. The first practical aviator seems to have been a Greek named Achytas, and we are told he invented a dove of wood propelled by heated air. There is another ancient record of a brass fly which made a short flight, so that we may be sure that even the ancients had their own ideas about heavier-than-air machines.

As far as we may judge from these quaint old records the early aviators attempted to fly with wings which they flapped about them in imitation of birds. About the year 67 A. D., during the reign of the Emperor Nero, an aviator named " Simon the Magician " made a public flight before a Roman crowd. According to the record, " He rose into the air through the assistance of demons. But St. Peter having offered a prayer, the action of the demons ceased and the magician was crushed in a fall and perished instantly." The end of the account, which sounds very probable indeed, is the first aëronautical smash-up on record.

MODEL AEROPLANES

Even in these early days the interest in aëronautics appears to have been widespread. It is recorded that a British king named Baldud succeeded in flying over the city of Trinovante, but unfortunately fell and, landing on a temple, was instantly killed. In the eleventh century a Benedictine monk built a pair of wings modelled upon the poet Ovid's description of those used by Daedalus, which was apparently a very uncertain model. The aviator jumped from a high tower against the wind, and, according to the record, sailed for 125 feet, when he fell and broke both his legs. That he should have attempted to fly against the wind, by the way, indicates some knowledge of aircraft.

If we may trust the rude folklore of the Middle Ages, the glider form of airship which anticipated the modern aëroplane was used with some success a thousand years ago. An inventor named Oliver of Malmesburg, built a glider and soared for 370 feet, which would be a creditable record for such a craft even in our day.

A hundred years later a Saracen attempted to fly in the same way and was killed by a fall. The number of men who have given their lives to the cause of aviation in all these centuries of experiment must be considerable.

Meanwhile the kite and balloon had long been in use in China. There is no reason to doubt that kites were well understood and even put to practical use in time of war as early as 300 B. C. A Chinese general, Han Sin, is said to have actually signalled by kites to a beleaguered city that he was outside the walls and expected to lend assistance. And a French missionary visiting China in 1694 reported that he had seen the records of the coronation of the Emperor Fo Kien in 1306 which described the balloon ascensions that formed part of the ceremony.

The fifteenth century was the most active period in aëronautical experiments before our own. A number of intelligent minds worked at the problem and notable progress was made, although all fell short of flying. Even in the light of our present knowledge of aëronautics we must admire the thorough, scientific way the aviators went about their work five centuries ago. Many of their discoveries have been of great assistance to our modern aviators. Had these investigators possessed our modern machinery, of which they knew little or nothing, it is, very likely they would actually have flown.

One of the greatest of these investigators was Leonardo da Vinci, famous as architect and engineer as well as painter and sculptor. To begin at the beginning of the subject, he dissected the bodies of many birds and made careful, technical drawings to illustrate the theory of the action of wings. These drawings and descriptions are still preserved, and even to-day repay careful study. He also calculated with great detail the amount of force which would be necessary to drive such machines. Plans were prepared for flying machines of the heavier than air form to be driven by wings, and even by screw pro-

A Serviceable Form Made of Wire.

pellers, which was looking far into the future.

Among all these early experiments the best record of actual flight was made by Batitta Dante, a brother of the great Italian poet. In 1456 Dante flew in a glider of his own construction for more than 800 feet at Perugia in Italy and a few years later he succeeded in flying in the same glider over Lake Trasimene. The glides made by the Wright Brothers while perfecting their machines seldom reached this length.

For several centuries it was believed that a lifting screw, if one could be built, would supply enough lifting power to support a heavier than air machine. Da Vinci experimented along this line for many years and even built a number of models with paper screws. This form of flying machine is called the helicopter. The plan was then abandoned for nearly five centuries and revived in our own century. The record of all the aviators and their experiments would fill many volumes.

MODEL AEROPLANES

The belief that man could learn to fly by flapping wings up and down was not given up until very recently. Nearly all the early machines were built on this principle. Man can never fly as the birds do because his muscles are differently grouped. In the birds the strongest muscles, the driving power, are in the chest at the base of the wings where they are most needed. It is amusing to find that while the birds are always flying before our eyes no one has guessed their secrets. Many attempts have been made to wrest their secrets from them by attaching dynometers to their wings to measure the force of the muscles but little has been learned in this way. One scientist calculated that a goose exerts 200 horse power while another investigator figured out that it was one tenth of one horse power. Many of the theories of flight have been quite as far apart. A great variety of false notions about flying had to be tried and from all these failures man slowly learned the road he must follow.

CHAPTER II

THE opening of the twentieth century found the world well prepared for actual conquest of the air. Aviation has been developed to an exact science. It had taken centuries of failure to teach man that he could not fly by flapping his wings like the birds but the idea was at last abandoned. The birds were still the models of the heavier-than-air machines, but man had at last learned to study them more intelligently. The marvellous development of modern mechanics, especially the building of light and efficient motors, was also of great importance. The theory of the aëroplane was rapidly gaining in favor.

It was thought at one time that since no birds weighed more than fifty pounds no flying machine heavier than this could ever fly. Some years ago Hiram S. Maxim pointed out, however, that if we had built our steam engines to imitate the horse, as we then hoped to build flying machines like the birds, we would have built locomotives which weighed only five tons, the weight of an elephant, which walked five miles an hour. The secret of flight evidently did not lie in closely imitating the familiar forms of flight. So far as man was interested it lay clearly in the soaring flights. When a bird flies with extended wings it does two things. It forms an aëroplane which supports its body, much the same as a kite, and it operates a propeller for driving this aëroplane forward. And so men finally learned to fly by borrowing a single principle from the birds.

It is claimed by some that the theory, and largely the form, of the modern successful aëroplane was first suggested by an English inventor, Sir George Cayley, as early as 1796. Cayley argued that a flat plane or surface when driven through the air inclined slightly upward would lift a considerable weight. He also suggested that a tail would help to steady the plane as well as steer it upward or downward. His ideas of propelling the aëroplane by screws driven by motors was also far in advance of his time, but the engines then in existence were much too heavy for the purpose and he never built a model.

Fifty years later, when the steam engine had been highly developed, these old plans were remembered and two engineers, Hensen and Stringfellow, actually built a flying machine on Cayley's principles. This early aëroplane was of the monoplane form, made of oiled silk stretched over a frame of bamboo. A car to carry a steam engine, and presumably the passengers, was hung below this plane. The motive power was supplied by two propellers at the rear. The aëroplane carried a fanshaped tail with a rudder for steering it sideways, placed beneath. The model is said to have actually flown for a short distance, but proved to be unstable.

From this time onward the experiments

became more scientific and accurate. Reliable scientific data was accumulated which later enabled the aviators to build practical aëroplanes. A number of interesting experiments were made shortly afterward by a scientist named Wenham to prove that the lifting powers of a carrying surface might be increased by arranging small surfaces in tiers one above another. Wenham had watched the birds to some purpose, and decided that a single plane, large enough to support a man would be too large to control, but that a number of small surfaces would make the bird flight possible. Wenham built and patented a machine in 1866. He never flew but he collected a great deal of valuable information about the behavior of planes.

The slow, but on the whole, encouraging movement toward the successful flying machine was given a serious set back in 1872 by a book written by H. Von Humboldt announcing the result of his experiments. This well known scientist, whose

PLATE XIV.

The Under Body of the Monoplane Shown, Plate XIII.

name carried great weight, wrote that mechanical flight was impossible. He based his idea on the discovery that as the body increased in size the work or power required to lift it increased more rapidly than the size of the body. In other words, a very large bird or flying machine could not contain muscles strong enough or machinery strong enough to enable it to fly. He argued that no bird larger than the albatross, for instance had ever lived, therefore no flying machines could ever be more than toys. The book was so discouraging that many aviators gave up their experiments and the science of aviation stood still.

It may be said to have been awakened, however, by the German scientist, Otto Lilenthal, whose book, published in 1886, at once attracted world wide attention. It was this book, incidentally, which inspired the Wright Brothers to begin their experiments. Lilenthal was not only a great scientist, but he worked on the principle that an ounce of actual experience was worth a ton of theory. In aviation, where the weight is all important, this saving was naturally of the greatest importance. Lilenthal built gliders, many of them, and put to actual test the theories which others had merely talked and figured about. Finally he set up an engine on a glider but the machine turned over and he was instantly killed. The scientific information he collected, however, proved of the highest value to those who later actually conquered the air.

Lilenthal built a hill fifty feet in height and shaped like a cone with sides slanting at an angle of thirty degrees. Here he proved by actual tests that he might fly no matter which way the wind blew and that an arched surface, driven against the wind, would rise from the ground and support his weight. A great deal of scientific information was collected and tabulated as well as the exact effect of the pressure of the air. He also changed the shape of the gliding surfaces, making them very long and narrow and driving them edge-

wise as in the first form of aëroplane. The aëroplane took shape in his hands. The success of these experiments encouraged aviators in many countries to imitate him, and so great was the interest aroused that even his fatal accident in 1896 did not discourage them. The successful flying machine was now actually in sight.

For a time it was believed that Hiram S. Maxim would be the first to construct a flying machine which would actually fly. He had gone about the problem in a thoroughly scientific manner, sparing neither time nor expense. An elaborate apparatus was first constructed like a revolving derrick, to test accurately the lifting powers of various aëroplanes of various sizes and shapes flying at different angles, as well as the propelling force of many kinds of screws. The horizontal arm of this machine was thirty feet, nine inches long, so that it described a circle of 200 feet in circumference. The arm was driven by an engine at high speed.

The various aëroplane forms to be tested

were attached to the extreme end of this arm, and driven by propellers of various shapes and sizes, exactly as they would be in actual flight. Every part of the machine, meanwhile, was so adjusted that the readings of the speed of the aëroplane, its lifting power, the exact force of the propeller, in fact, every detail, could be measured and recorded with scientific accuracy. This preliminary work proved to be of the highest value. The test showed, for instance, just what size the propeller should be for different size planes, and the exact pitch of the screw which would give the best results, the proper angle of elevation for the front plane, the resistance offered by various shaped planes, and the exact amount of power required for planes of different sizes. A delicate machine was also built to test the different kinds of fabrics used for covering the planes. The fabric was stretched over a small steel frame, mounted at a slight angle, in a blast of air. The tendency of the cloth to lift or drift was then accurately measured.

The material which gave the greatest amount of lift and the least drift was used.

A large aëroplane was finally built in 1893. It weighed 7500 pounds, measured 104 feet in width, and was driven by a 360 horsepower engine. Compared with the clear cut, ship-shape air-craft of to-day this early model appears crude and cumbersome. The main plane was almost square in shape, while stability planes extended out from the sides. A series of four narrow planes, one above another, were carried below on either side. The machinery for driving was carried far below the main plane. The two large propellers were placed in the stern. The aëroplane was run along a double-tracked railroad 1800 feet in length, to gather sufficient momentum to cause it to rise. Almost any school-boy of to-day familiar with the aëroplane models could have told at a glance that the machine could not rise. When it was finally sent down the track at a good clip, the front wheels did actually rise a trifle but it immediately came down with a bad smash.

Not in the least discouraged, Maxim at once designed a new machine. This measured fifty feet in width and forty feet in length in the middle, but with the corners cut off, so that it was sharpened both fore and aft. The wings were made long and narrow, extending out twenty-seven feet beyond the main plane, and large fore and aft rudders were attached. It was not even expected that the machine would fly. All that was hoped for was that it would lift somewhat so that its upward tendency might be accurately measured.

The most successful " flight " of this model will seem a very tame affair indeed to the boys of to-day who are daily reading of the marvellous voyages in air across sea and land. The " airship " was run over its track and the steam pressure run up to 329 pounds per square inch. The speed increased and the upward thrust began to be felt. Finally the front wheels of the machine actually lifted from the

PLATE XVI.

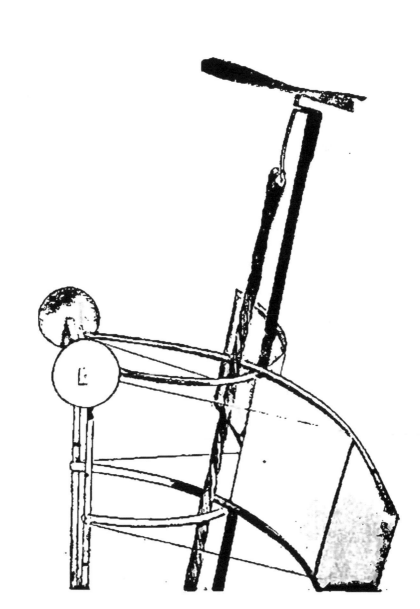

The Propeller and Shaft of the Model Shown, Plate XV.

track. The rear axle rose three or four feet above its normal position. When it alighted, the delighted aëronauts found that the wheels of the machine had passed over the turf for a very short distance, without making any marks, showing that for a second or so the machine was actually off the earth. It seems curious to us to-day that this " flight " should have been considered remarkable.

The experiments carried out by S. P. Langley, beginning in 1887 and lasting for four years, placed a great deal of valuable, scientific data in the hands of the aviators. Thousands of tests were made with an apparatus similar to that used by Maxim. In one class of these experiments solid metal planes were attached to the end of the revolving arm in such a way that they were free to fall for a fixed distance. When in rapid, horizontal motion, the metal seemed to part with its weight, and the material, though one thousand times heavier than the air, was found to be actually supported by it. It was proven, for instance, that one horse power would support over 200 pounds weight of planes driven at a speed of fifty miles an hour.

All this preliminary work, or nearly all, we now see, was necessary before a practical aëroplane could be constructed. The early aviators, although they did not fly, at least showed what not to do, and several paid the price of their lives for this knowledge. Lilenthal had mapped out the aëroplane in the rough, and determined the general shape it must take. The experiments of Maxim and Langley enabled the successful aviators to calculate the size of the machine necessary to carry them and the amount of power required to drive it.

CHAPTER III

THE Wright Brothers brought to their work a genius for invention and, making free use of the results of former investigation and experiment, finally succeeded in building a heavier than air machine which would actually fly. The story of their experiments and final success, which one may read in their own words, forms one of the most fascinating chapters in the history of invention.

The Wright Brothers' first flying machine was a mere toy. "Late in the autumn of 1878" they tell the story, "our father came into the house one evening with some object partially concealed in his hands, and before we could see what it was, he tossed it into the air. Instead of falling to the floor, as we expected, it flew across the room till it struck the ceiling, where it fluttered for a while, and finally sank to the floor. It was a little toy known to scientists as a 'hélicoptère' but which we, with sublime disregard for science, dubbed a bat. It was a light frame of cork and bamboo which formed two screws driven in opposite directions by rubber bands under torsion. A toy so delicate lasted only a short time in the hands of small boys, but its memory was abiding."

The interest of the brothers in aëronautics was awakened. "We began building these hélicoptères ourselves," their story goes on, "making each one larger than that preceding. But, to our astonishment, we found that the larger the 'bat,' the less it flew. We did not know that a machine having only twice the linear dimensions of another would require eight times the power. We finally became discouraged, and returned to kite-flying, a sport to which we had devoted so much attention that we were regarded as experts. But as we became older, we had to give up this

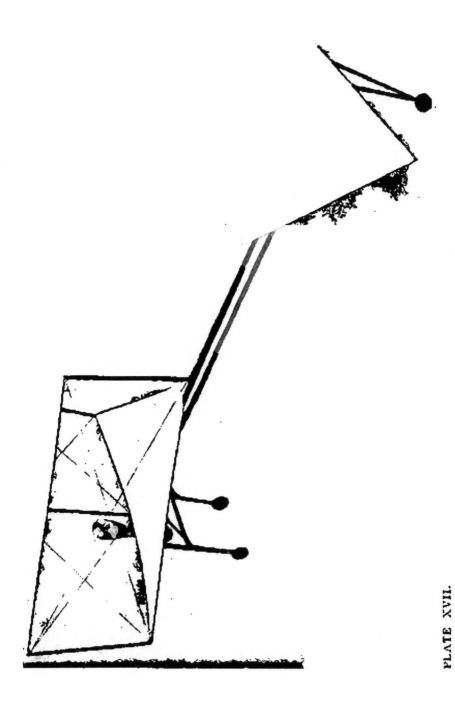

PLATE XVII.

An Ingenious Model which Fails to Fly.

fascinating sport as unbecoming to boys of our age."

The Wrights did not begin their experiments until the summer of 1896. They first prepared themselves thoroughly by reading the literature on aëronautics, making themselves familiar with the results of all the experimental work of the aviators — Langley, Chanute, Mouillard, and others. The Wrights soon decided that the first thing to be solved was to build aëroplanes which would fly and that, until this was solved, it was foolish to waste time building delicate and costly machinery to operate them. They took up the problems of the glider and sought by actual tests what many scientists had been theorizing about for years.

They soon discarded the various forms of gliders then used for experiments. The tests which led up to adopting the now famous Wright model, the basis for all heavier than air machines to-day, occupied very little time. The story of this marvellous discovery which will rank with that of Robert Fulton or Watt, is best told in their own words, which are here somewhat abbreviated.

" The balancing of a flier may seem, at first thought, to be a very simple matter," say the Wrights, "yet almost every experimenter had found in this the point he could not satisfactorily master. Many different methods were tried. Some experimenters place the center of gravity far below the wings in the belief that the wings would naturally seek to remain at the lowest point. A more satisfactory system, especially for lateral balance, was that of arranging the wings in the shape of a broad V to form a dihedral angle, with the center low and the wing-tips elevated. In theory this was an automatic action, but in practice it had two serious defects; first, it tended to keep the machine oscillating; and, second, its usefulness was restricted to calm air. Notwithstanding the known limitations of this principle, it had been embodied in almost every prominent flying-machine which had been built.

" We reached the conclusion that such machines might be of interest from a scientific point of view, but could be of no value in a practical way. We, therefore, resolved to try a fundamentally different principle. We would arrange the flyer so that it would not tend to right itself. We would make it as inert as possible to the effects of change of direction or speed, and thus reduce the effects of wind-gusts to a minimum. We would do this in the fore-and-aft stability by giving the aëroplanes a peculiar shape; and in the lateral balance, by arching the surfaces from tip to tip, just the reverse of what our predecessors had done. Then by some suitable contrivance, actuated by the operator, forces should be brought into play to regulate the balance."

" Lilenthal and Chanute had guided and balanced their machines by shifting the weight of the operator's body. But this method seemed to us incapable of expansion to meet large conditions, because the weight to be moved and the distance of possible motion were limited, while the disturbing forces steadily increased, both with wing area and wind velocity. In order to meet the needs of large machines, we wished to employ some system whereby the operator could vary at will the inclination of different parts of the wings, and thus obtain from the wind forces to restore the balance which wind itself had disturbed. This could easily be done by using wings capable of being warped, and adjustable surfaces in the shape of rudders. A happy device was discovered whereby the surfaces could be so warped that aëroplanes could be presented on the right and left sides at different angles to the wind. This, with an adjustable horizontal front rudder, formed the main features of our first glider."

"We began our first active experiments at the close of this period, in October, 1900, at Kitty Hawk, North Carolina. Our machine was designed to be flown as a kite, with a man on board, in winds of from fifteen to twenty miles an hour. But, upon trial, it was found that much stronger winds were required to lift it. Suitable winds not being plentiful, we found it necessary, in order to test the new balancing system, to fly the machine as a kite without a man on board, operating the levers through cords from the ground. This did not give the practice anticipated, but it inspired confidence in the new system of balance."

"The machine of 1901 was built with the shape of surface used by Lilenthal, curved from front to rear, with a slight curvature of $\frac{41}{12}$ of its cord. But to make doubly sure that it would have sufficient lifting capacity when flown as a kite in fifteen or twenty mile winds, we increased the area from 165 square feet, used in 1900, to 308 square feet, a size much larger than Lilenthal, Chanute, or Pilcher had deemed safe. Upon trial, however, the lifting capacity again fell short of calculation, so that the idea of securing practice while flying as a kite, had to be abandoned. Mr.

Chanute, who witnessed the experiments, told us that the trouble was not due to poor construction of the machine. We saw only one other explanation — that the tables of air pressure in general use were incorrect."

" We then turned to gliding — coasting down hill in the air — as the only method of getting the desired practice in balancing the machine. After a few minutes' practice we were able to make glides of 300 feet, and in a few days were safely operating in twenty-seven mile winds. In these experiments we met with several unexpected phenomena. We found that, contrary to the teachings of the books, the center of pressure on a curved surface traveled backward when the surface was inclined, at small angles, more and more edgewise to the wind. We also discovered that in free flight, when the wing on one side of the machine was presented to the wind at a greater angle than the one on the other side, the wing with the greater angle descended, and the machine turned in a direction just the reverse of what we were led to expect when flying the machine as a kite. The larger angle gave more resistance to forward motion, and reduced the speed of the wing on that side. The decrease in speed more than counterbalanced the effect of the larger angle. The addition of a fixed vertical vane in the rear increased the trouble, and made the machine absolutely dangerous. It was some time before a remedy was discovered. This consisted of movable rudders working in conjunction with the twisting of the wings."

"The experiments of 1901 were far from encouraging. We saw that the calculations upon which all flying-machines had been based were unreliable, and that all were simply groping in the dark. Having set out with absolute faith in the existing scientific data, we were driven to doubt one thing after another, till finally, after two years of experiment, we cast it all aside, and decided to rely entirely upon our own investigations. Truth and error

were everywhere so intimately mixed as
to be indistinguishable. Nevertheless, the
time expended in preliminary study of
books was not misspent, for they gave us
a good general understanding of the subject, and enabled us at the outset to avoid
effort in many directions in which results
would have been hopeless."

"To work intelligently, one needs to
know the effects of a multitude of varia-
tions that would be incorporated in the
surfaces of flying-machines. The pres-
sures on squares are different from those
on rectangles, circles, triangles, or ellipses;
arched surfaces differ from planes, and
vary among themselves according to the
depth of curvature; true arcs differ from
parabolas, and the latter differ among
themselves; thick surfaces differ from
thin, and surfaces thicker in one place
than another vary in pressure when the
positions of maximum thickness are different; some surfaces are more efficient
at one angle, others at other angles. The
shape of the edge also makes a difference,

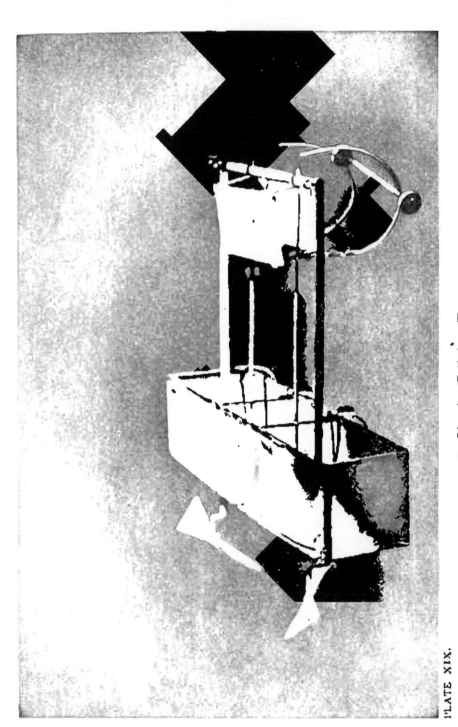

PLATE XIX.

A Simple Cellular Form.

so that thousands of combinations are possible in so simple a thing as a wing."

"We had taken aëronautics merely as a sport. We reluctantly entered upon the scientific side of it. But we soon found the work so fascinating that we were drawn into it deeper and deeper. Two testing machines were built, which we believed would avoid the errors to which the measurements of others had been subject, after making preliminary measurements on a great number of different-shaped surfaces, so varied in design as to bring out the underlying causes of difference noted in their pressure. Measurements were tabulated on nearly fifty of these at all angles from zero to 45 degrees.

"In September and October, 1902, nearly one thousand flights were made, several of which covered distances of over 600 feet. Some, made against a wind of thirty-six miles an hour, gave proof of the effectiveness of the devices for control. With this machine, in the autumn of 1903, we made a number of flights in which we remained in the air for over a minute, after soaring for a considerable time in one spot, without any descent at all. Little wonder that our unscientific assistant should think the only thing needed to keep it indefinitely in the air would be a coat of feathers to make it light."

"With accurate data for making calculations, and a system of balance effective in winds as well as in calms, we were now in a position, we thought, to build a successful power-flyer. The first designs proved for a total weight of 600 pounds, including the operator and an eight horsepower motor. But, upon completion, the motor gave more power than had been estimated, and this allowed 150 pounds to be added for strengthening the wings and other parts.

"It was not till several months had passed, and every phase of the problem had been thrashed over and over, that the various reactions began to untangle themselves. When once a clear understanding had been obtained, there was no difficulty in designing suitable propellers, with proper diameter, pitch, and area of blade, to meet the requirements of the flyer. High efficiency in a screw propeller is not dependent upon any particular or peculiar shape, and there is no such thing as a 'best' screw. A propeller giving a high dynamic efficiency when used upon one machine, may be almost worthless when used upon another. The propeller should in every case be designed to meet the particular conditions of the machine to which it is to be applied. Our first propellers, built entirely from calculation, gave in useful work 66 per cent of the power expended. This was about one third more than had been secured by Maxim and Langley."

"The first flights with the power-machine were made on the 17th of December, 1903. The first flight lasted only twelve seconds, a flight very modest compared with that of birds, but it was, nevertheless, the first in the history of the world in which a machine carrying a man had raised itself by its own power into the air in free flight, had sailed forward on a level course without reduction of speed, and had finally landed without being wrecked. The second and third flights were a little longer, and the fourth lasted fifty-nine seconds, covering a distance of 853 feet over the ground against a twenty-mile wind."

"After the last flight, the machine was carried back to camp and set down in what was thought to be a safe place. But a few minutes later, when engaged in conversation about the flights, a sudden gust of wind struck the machine, and started to turn it over. All made a rush to stop it, but we were too late. Mr. Daniels, a giant in stature and strength, was lifted off his feet, and falling inside, between the surfaces, was shaken about like a rattle in a box as the machine rolled over and over. He finally fell out upon the sand with nothing worse than painful bruises, but the damage to the machine caused a discontinuance of experiments.

PLATE XX.

A Cellular Type with Rudder and Elevating Plane

THE WRIGHT BROTHERS' STORY

"In the spring of 1904, through the kindness of Mr. Torrence Huffman of Dayton, Ohio, we were permitted to erect a shed, and to continue experiments, on what is known as the Huffman Prairie, at Simms Station, eight miles east of Dayton. The new machine was heavier and stronger, but similar to the one flown at Kitty Hawk. When preparations had been completed, a wind of three or four miles was blowing, — insufficient for starting on so short a track, — but since many had come a long way to see the machine in action an attempt was made. To add to the other difficulty, the engine refused to work properly. The machine, after running the length of the track, slid off the end without rising in the air at all. Several of the newspaper men returned the next day, but were again disappointed. The engine performed badly, and after a glide of only sixty feet, the machine came to the ground. Further trial was postponed till the motor could be put in better running condition.

MODEL AEROPLANES

"We had not been flying long in 1904 before we found that the problem of equilibrium had not as yet been entirely solved. Sometimes, in making a circle, the machine would turn over sidewise despite anything the operator could do, although, under the same conditions in ordinary flight, it could have been righted in an instant. In one flight, in 1905, while circling about a honey-locust tree at a height of about fifty feet, the machine suddenly began to turn up on one wing, and took a course toward the tree. The operator, not relishing the idea of landing in a thorn tree, attempted to reach the ground. The left wing, however, struck the tree at a height of ten or twelve feet from the ground, and carried away several branches; but the flight, which had covered a distance of six miles, was continued to the starting point.

"The causes of these troubles — too technical for explanation here — were not entirely overcome till the end of September, 1905. The flights then rapidly increased in length, till experiments were discontinued after the 5th of October.

"A practical flyer having been finally realized, we spent the years 1906 and 1907 in constructing new machines and in business negotiations. It was not till May of this year (1908) that experiments were resumed at Kill Devil Hill, North Carolina. The recent flights were made to test the ability of our machines to meet the requirements of a contract with the United States Government to furnish a flier capable of carrying two men and sufficient fuel supplies for a flight of 125 miles, with a speed of forty miles an hour. The machine used in these tests was the one with which the flights were made at Simms Station in 1905, though several changes had been made to meet present requirements. The operator assumed a sitting position, instead of lying prone, as in 1905, and a seat was added for a passenger. A larger motor was installed, and radiators and gasolene reservoirs of larger capacity replaced those previously used."

MODEL AEROPLANES

Let us now take a short air journey with one of the Wright Brothers as pilot. He describes the experience as follows, " Let us fancy ourselves ready for the start. The machine is placed on a single rail track facing the wind and is securely fastened with a cable. The engine is put in motion, and the propellers in the rear whirr. You take your seat at the center of the machine beside the operator. He slips the cable, and you shoot forward. An assistant who has been holding the machine in balance on the rail, starts forward with you, but before you have gone fifty feet the speed is too great for him, and he lets go. Before reaching the end of the track the operator moves the front rudder, and the machine lifts from the rail like a kite supported by the pressure of the air underneath. The ground under you is at first a perfect blur, but as you rise the objects become clearer. At a height of one hundred feet you feel hardly any motion at all, except for the wind which strikes your face. If you did not

A Complicated Model Capable of Long Flights.

PLATE XXI.

take the precaution to fasten your hat before starting, you have probably lost it by this time. The operator moves a lever; the right wing rises and the machine swings about to the left. You make a very short turn, yet you do not feel the sensation of being thrown from your seat, so often experienced in automobile and railway travel. You find yourself facing toward the point from which you started. The objects on the ground seem to be moving at much higher speed, though you perceive no change in the pressure of wind in your face. You know then that you are traveling with the wind. When you near the starting point, the operator stops the motor while still high in the air. The machine coasts down at an oblique angle to the ground, and after sliding fifty or a hundred feet, comes to rest. Although the machine often lands when traveling at a speed of a mile a minute, you feel no shock whatever, and cannot in fact, tell the exact moment at which it first touched the ground. The motor close beside you kept up an almost deafening roar during the whole flight, yet in your excitement, you did not notice it till it stopped."

On his return from Le Mans Mr. Wilbur Wright estimated that during a single year he had flown upwards of 3000 miles. With the memory of these marvellous flights in his mind he described his sensations to the present writer with enthusiasm.

"Flying is the greatest sport in the world," says Mr. Wilbur Wright. "I can't describe the sensation, I can only define it by comparison with more familiar experiences. It is like sledding, like motoring, like sailing, but with increased exhilaration and freedom.

"An aëroplane flight, contrary to the general impression, is far steadier than the familiar means of locomotion. There is absolute freedom from the bouncing of the automobile, the jar of a railroad train, or the rolling and pitching sensations of the sea. No matter how many springs or cushions may be added to the automobile, for instance, there will always be some motion. On the other hand, the seat of an aëroplane is always steady. The aëroplane does not jolt over the invisible wind currents, the ruts of the sky. It cuts its way smoothly. Even suppose the plane to be gliding so (indicating an angle of forty-five degrees), the seat remains fixed. There is, of course, no absolute parallel in surface travel. And since there is no roll or pitch to the aëroplane, there is no air-sickness comparable to the familiar sea sickness."

CHAPTER IV

ABOARD THE WRIGHTS' AIRSHIP

SEEN high aloft the Wright aëroplane appears so graceful and fragile that its actual dimensions come as a surprise. In the upper air it seems no larger than a swallow, but, as it settles to earth, the wings lengthen out to the width of an ordinary street.

There is some good reason for each stick and wire, and for every twist and turn of the Wrights' marvellous airship. When one considers what wonderful feats this aircraft performs, its form and mechanism seem extremely simple. It is far less complicated than any locomotive or steamship, and the action of its planes is far easier to explain than the sails of an ordinary sea-going ship. When one has once gone over the fascinating little craft, all other aëro-

PLATE XXII.

An Interesting Form which Flies Backward or Forward.

planes, which more or less resemble it, may be readily understood.

The Wright machine was not only the first power airship to fly and carry a man aloft, but for all its rivals, it still rides the unstable air currents more steadily than any other. The planes measure forty feet from tip to tip, six and a half feet across, and are spaced six feet apart. The distance between the planes is very important and was only fixed after a number of experiments. The area of the wings or supporting surfaces is 540 feet, which is considerably more than in most airships. The machine complete, without any passenger or pilot, weighs 880 pounds, although you would imagine it to be much less. The two propellers measure eight feet in diameter, and turn at the rate of 450 revolutions a minute. Equipped with a four cylinder engine of from 25 to 30 horse power, the airship has a speed of forty miles an hour, which is often increased when traveling with the wind.

The seats for the pilot and the passenger are placed at the center at the front of the lower plane, so that their feet hang over the front or entering edge. The passenger sits very comfortably throughout the flight. There is a back to lean against, a brace for the feet, while the struts between the planes give every opportunity to hold on. In some of the models these seats are even upholstered in gray to harmonize with the silver or aluminium paint of the machine.

A second and smaller biplane, which serves both as rudder and lifting plane, extends about ten feet in front of the main planes. These two planes, which have a combined area of eighty square feet, may be inclined upward or downward by touching a lever at the pilot's seat. The motor, radiator and petrol or fuel tank are placed on the lower plane in the center of the machine so that they balance the weight of the pilot and the passenger. The weight of the lifting planes and rudders rests on the main planes or lower deck.

The most interesting feature of the

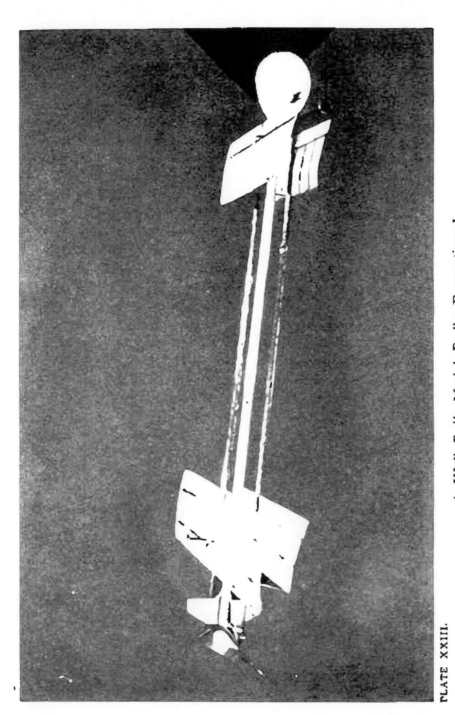

PLATE XXIII.

A Well Built Model Badly Proportioned

Wrights' airship is, of course, the method for flexing the tips of the wings or planes to imitate the flight of the birds. The ends of the large planes are made slightly flexible, and may be turned up or down by moving a lever placed convenient to the pilot's hand. Both planes are flexed, or turned up or down, at the same time the vertical rudder moves, so that, when the aëroplane turns to right or left, the wings give the machine the proper balance. If it were not for this arrangement, the ends of the planes in turning would tend to rise, since they travel the faster, and the machine would be in danger of upsetting. The ends of the planes may also be flexed separately when the machine is in straight flight, whenever it becomes necessary to balance it against a dangerous air current or a gust of wind. The pilot, it will be seen, has every point of the great machine, as it were, at his finger ends.

The marvellous power placed in the hands of the pilot of one of these models makes him almost equal of the birds soaring about him. Let us suppose an accident to occur. Even should the engine stop, the skillful pilot is still master of the situation. He can actually coast down to the ground on the air with comparative safety. Mr. Orville Wright has soared up 3000 feet and, after stopping his propeller, slid down on nothing at all, at the rate of more than twenty miles an hour, by the force of gravity alone.

The Wright method of alighting is also borrowed from the birds. Watch any bird alight on a twig, and you will see that it always settles on the top of the twig, which is pressed straight down by its weight, and never sideways. As the Wrights come down, they approach to within a few feet of the earth, but, without touching they swoop up again, and finally settle down from a height of only a few feet. Considering the weight of their machine, they actually come down as lightly as a bird. While traveling at a speed of forty miles an hour they will skid along the ground or come to rest within five or six feet, so quietly that a passenger cannot tell when he lands.

No part of the aëroplane calls for more clever workmanship than the wings or planes. They must be so thin and light that they will ride the air like the wings of a bird, and yet strong enough to support the weight of hundreds of pounds of machinery and of passengers. In the Wright model, the planes are made entirely of wood, but so ingeniously braced that they are perfectly rigid. The building of such a wing is especially difficult, since it must be curved with scientific accuracy. In the Wright model machines, as in all aëroplanes, the curve is upward, with the highest point of the arch near the front or entering edge.

Both sides of the frame are completely covered so that they may offer the least possible amount of resistance. There is not a ridge, scarcely a seam, to catch the air. A stout canvas is used for covering. The ingenuity of these clever workmen led them to lay on the cloth with the thread running diagonally, at an angle of forty-five degrees. This plan serves to hold the frame more closely together and keeps the cloth from bagging or wrinkling.

At the first glance, the Wright machine appears to be made entirely of aluminium. Seen high aloft in the sunlight, it appears like some delicate jewel. The effect is due to the paint. The entire framework of the machine is made of spruce pine except the curved part of the wings, or entering edge, which is of ash. The propellers are driven by chains, connected with the motor, which run in steel tubes, thus doing away with the danger of fouling by passengers or loose objects. The ignition system is operated by a high tension Eisenmann magneto machine. The petrol used for fuel is carried in a tank placed above the engines and is supplied by gravity. The two wings are connected by a series of distance rods and wire cross-stays, which keep the entire front, or entering edge, and central part of the model, perfectly rigid.

PLATE XXIV.

A Wright Model Ready for Flight.

ABOARD THE WRIGHTS' AIRSHIP

Although nearly all the aëroplanes, nowadays, are mounted on ordinary bicycle wheels, the Wrights prefer a simple system of skids, not unlike the runners of a sleigh. One of the great advantages of the skids is the fact that they take up the shock on landing more completely than wheels and protect the machine from many a hard bump.

The airship rests on a small frame mounted on two wheels, placed tandem, and is balanced on a small trolley which runs along a rail about twenty-five feet in length. It is started by the pull of a rope attached to a 1500 pound weight, which drops from a derrick fifteen feet in height. When everything is ready, the temporary wheels are taken away, the rope is attached, and finally the weight released. The machine glides swiftly down the track, and when the necessary speed has been reached, the pilot raises his elevating planes, a trifle, and the ship glides gracefully upward and onward.

CHAPTER V

IN the summer of 1904 the boys of Paris were greatly interested in watching a curious, giant kite in flight over the River Seine. The string of this kite was drawn by a fast motor boat, which darted along, while the kite rose high in the air. Its inventor tinkered with it, and changed its wings about until it finally flew like no other kite ever seen in France. All this was by no means mere play, however, for many scientists watched the kite as it soared about and a great deal of valuable information about the behavior of kites of this shape was learned. The man with the kite, who soon became famous in the world of aviation, was named Voisin. The aëroplane, which he afterwards built, modeled on this kite, was flown in many

238

remarkable flights by Henry Farman, Delagrange, Paulhan, and others. Like the Wright airship, Voisin's is a biplane or double plane model.

Although at first glance, the Voisin and Wright aëroplanes may seem very much alike, as we look more closely, we will find many points of contrast. The Voisin model has a large tail-piece, consisting of two vertical planes, which project far behind. These planes are believed to make its flight very steady. A single vertical rudder is placed between the two rear edges of this plane. The rudders are turned by horizontal, sliding bars attached to the wheels, directly before the pilot's seat, like an automobile. The horizontal rudder in front, which corresponds to the Wrights' double lifting plane, is single and is placed lower down than in the Wright model.

The steadiness of the Voisin aëroplane in flight is gained without flexing the planes. A series of four vertical planes connect the upper and lower wings which give the machine much the appearance of a box kite. These walls are arranged so that the space enclosed at either end is almost square. It is believed that the arrangement of these walls keeps the air from sliding off the under surface of the horizontal planes, and thus greater lifting power is obtained. It is claimed that the model has much greater longitudinal stability than the Wrights' machine. In other words, the long tail piece prevents the machine from tipping or pitching when the wind gusts come unevenly. The box-like or cellular form, it is believed also, adds to its stability. The model holds the record for flying at the lowest speed — 22.8 miles an hour. On the other hand, the Voisin model cannot, with any degree of safety, coast down on the air from great altitudes, like the Wright model.

The method of starting the Voisin airship is entirely different from the Wrights'. The machine is mounted on two wheels, attached to the girder body with an arrangement of springs to take up the shock on landing. To launch the aëroplane, the propellers are started, and the machine rushes forward on its wheels until it has developed sufficient speed to send it up. It may thus rise from an ordinarily level ground, and does not require the apparatus used by the Wrights. The pilot and passenger sit in much the same position as in the Wright aëroplane.

The Voisin model weighs 300 pounds more than the Wrights' or 1590 pounds. It has a supporting surface of 535 square feet, and a speed, under favorable conditions, of 38 miles an hour. Another point of difference from the Wright model is the propeller, which is single and measures seven feet six inches in diameter. The motor, an eight cylinder Antoinette, usually gives fifty horse power at 1100 revolutions per minute. The Wright Brothers, by the way, make their own motors, which are considered inferior to the French motors.

The smallest and swiftest of all the

aëroplanes is the Curtiss-Herring model, which was invented by two Americans whose names it bears. Its general form suggests the Wrights' machine. The span of the large planes is only 29 feet or under, the depth but four feet six inches, and the spacing four feet six inches. It has a total wing surface of but 258 square feet. The weight, not including the pilot, is only about 450 pounds. When seen beside the aëroplane of ordinary size, the little craft looks like a very large toy model. It has the appearance of a smart little racer, however, and its maximum speed is over 50 miles an hour.

Everything has been sacrificed in the Curtiss-Herring model for the sake of compactness. The forward rudder, which seems small even for such a craft, consists of two planes, one above the other, whose combined area is only twenty-four square feet. Unlike the Wright or Voisin models, this forward rudder carries a vertical plane which makes for stability. There is no tail as in the Voisin model, and the rear, vertical rudder consists of a horizontal plane six feet wide and two feet, three inches deep and a vertical rudder below it, two feet deep and three feet four inches wide. The front and rear planes extend out from the main frame about the same distance. The main stability planes, curiously enough, are placed inside the frame. There are two of these, one at either end of the main plane.

An ingenious method has been followed to control the various planes. The pilot sits facing a wheel, like that of an automobile, which is so rigged that by simply pushing it from him or pulling it back, he may lift or decline the front planes. By turning this wheel he operates the rudder in the rear, exactly as you would steer an automobile or a boat. The balancing mechanism in turn is connected with a frame which fits about the pilot's shoulders like a high-backed chair and is operated by merely leaning to one side or the other. This has the same effect as warping the main planes. The control of the machine becomes largely automatic. If the pilot feels that his aëroplane is tilting over at one end or the other, he merely leans to one side or the other, and, without taking his hands from the wheel before him, has the machine under perfect control. Even the motor is controlled by pedals placed under the pilot's feet.

This little racer is mounted on three wheels, one well forward and two in the rear about half way between the main planes and the horizontal rudder. An original feature of this model is a foot brake which, connecting with the forward wheel, helps to slow down the machine on landing, just as you close the brake of an automobile. There is only one rudder measuring six feet in diameter, which is unusually large considering the size of the model. The engine is mounted at the center of the space between the two main planes, and the propeller, which is kept on a line with it, is therefore considerably higher than in most aëroplanes. The lower plane comes very near the ground.

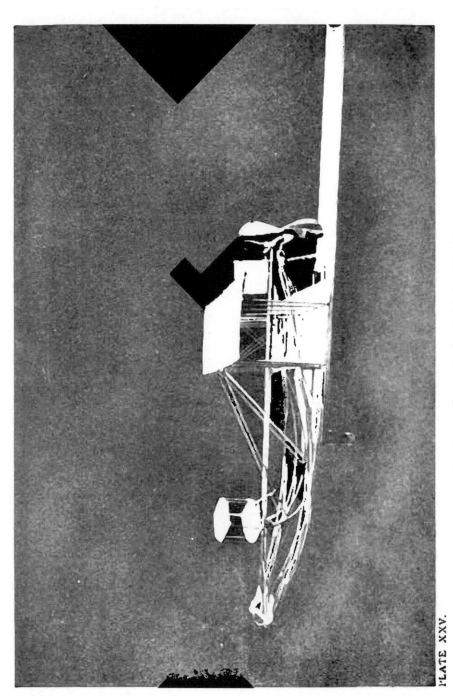

Another View of the Wright Model.

PLATE XXV.

It is only raised by about the height of the bicycle wheels. It is thought by some that this arrangement of the engine blankets the propeller, while others argue that the suction produced in this way increases the thrust of the propeller. The machine is built of Oregon spruce, the wings are covered with oiled rubber silk, and the entire mechanism is beautifully finished in every detail.

The ingenuity of the designers of aeroplanes is astonishing. With so many aeroplanes in the field, or rather in the sky, it is surprising that they are not more alike. The Farman biplane, for instance, follows the same general proportion as the Wright machine, but there the similarity ends. To secure equilibrium in this model, four small planes are used, hinged at the back of the two main planes, and these, it has been found, take the place of the flexing device used by the Wrights. The two swinging planes on the lower wing are controlled by wires, while the upper two swing free. A single lever controls the two lower planes and the horizontal rudder.

Farman has placed his rear stability planes unusually far behind the main frame. They consist of two fixed horizontal planes, one above the other, with a vertical rudder placed in the space between them. The front horizontal rudder for vertical steering, is . a single plane, mounted close to the entering edge. The vertical rudder is worked by a foot pedal. The machine is driven by one large wooden propeller, eight feet six inches in diameter, at a speed of 1300 revolutions per minute, which, it will be noticed, is unusually high. The Farman biplane is one of the heaviest yet constructed, weighing about 1000 pounds without the pilot.

An original plan has also been found for mounting the machine. The aëroplane rests upon a combination of skids and wheels. There are two sets of wheels under the front edge of the plane, while the two skids are placed between the wheels of each pair. The motor is four cylinder, fifty horse power type, and drives the machine at the rate of forty miles an hour.

The largest, and by far the heaviest aëroplane is the Cody biplane built by an American inventor who lives in England. It weighs nearly one ton, or more than 1800 pounds, to be exact, and measures fifty-two feet across. The machine is balanced somewhat after the manner of the Curtiss-Herring model, by two horizontal planes placed at the extremities of the main planes and midway between the rear corners. The two main planes are seven feet six inches wide and are placed nine feet apart, which is considerably farther than in any other successful model. The upper plane is slightly curved toward the ends. The machine carries two large horizontal planes for vertical steering, sixteen feet before the entering edge of the main wings. These planes, placed side by side, have a combined area of 150 square feet and naturally exert a considerable lifting force. A small vertical rudder for horizontal steering is carried above and between these front planes. An unusually large rudder is placed well behind the machine, consisting of a vertical plane with an area of forty square feet. All the rudders are operated by a wheel in front of the pilot's seat.

In the Cody aëroplane the horizontal rudders are moved by pushing or pulling the wheel, while by moving it sideways the two balancing planes, which control the equilibrium, are moved up and down. The most original feature of the Cody machine is the position of the propellers. They are carried in the space between the two main planes forward of the center. It would seem that they must draw the air from the upper planes and affect their lifting quality. The machine is mounted on three wheels, two beneath the front edge of the main plane, and the other slightly forward, which is an unusual distribution. The Cody biplane, with 770 feet of wing surface, lifts more than 1800 pounds.

It is all a matter of guess work, of

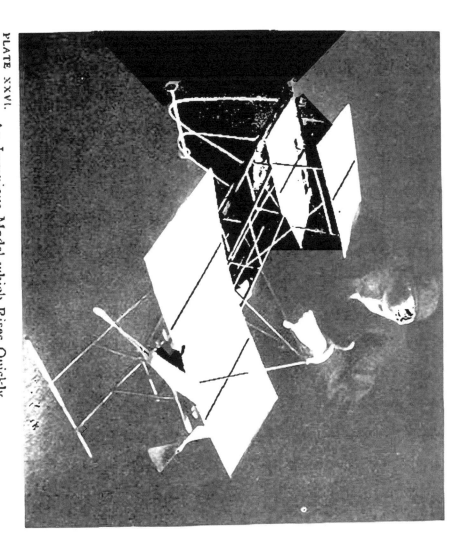

PLATE XXVI.   An Ingenious Model which Rises Quickly.

course, whether the monoplane, biplane, or some entirely new form of aëroplane will come into general use. Every model has its enthusiastic friends. The biplane, at present, has greater stability than the monoplane, and carries greater weights for longer distances. The development of the flying machine is so rapid however that in five or ten years the successful aëroplane models of to-day may appear as crude as do the clumsy, lumbering old horseless carriages of five or ten years ago.

CHAPTER VI

SUCCESSFUL MONOPLANES

WHILE the biplane borrows the general principles of flight from the birds, the monoplane carries us a step further and almost exactly reproduces their form and movement. Seen high aloft, with wings outspread, the monoplanes look like great eagles as, gracefully, but very noisily, they rise and fall in long, sweeping curves. The monoplane being a much lighter machine and less complicated is therefore cheaper to build than any multiplane model. Several of the successful models ride the air very steadily and have proven themselves capable of making long and difficult air journeys.

Some aviators believe that the monoplane type, highly developed, to be sure, will some day be adopted for great com-

PLATE XXVII.

An Aëroplane with Paper Wings.

mercial airships. Even in its present form, these mechanical birds look very shipshape. The pilot can find a more comfortable seat among these wings than in the biplane forms, and it takes little imagination to picture these airships, greatly enlarged, carrying comfortable cabins filled with air voyagers. The most successful model aëroplanes, by the way, are of the monoplane form.

The first monoplane to make an extended flight was the Bleriot. Its inventor had worked with Voisin in the experiments above the River Seine at Paris in 1906, and beginning with short flights of only a few yards worked his way step by step. The machine in which he crossed the English Channel in 1909, and made several remarkable cross country flights, was his eleventh model.

Bleriot's most successful model consists of only two wings curved upward, mounted on a long motor base which measures twenty-six and one half feet in length. The body of the monoplane, which is made of ash and poplar, tapers to a point in the rear and is partially covered with "Continental fabric," similar to balloons. The front or main wing is twenty-five and a half feet in width with a surface of 159 square feet. The rear plane measures only six feet in width, and three feet in depth and is equipped with moveable tips or horizontal rudders two feet square at either side. The vertical rudder for steering to right or left, is carried behind the frame. The planes are braced by a series of stay wires running in all directions.

Unlike the biplane, the motor of the monoplane is placed in front of the wings. The blades of the propeller, which are unusually broad, measure less than seven feet from tip to tip. The pilot's seat is inside the motor frame near the rear edge of the main wing, and with its high back and sides appears to be a comfortable place to sit. It has the disadvantage, however, of being directly behind the motor, so that a draft of air strikes the driver in the face.

The pilot keeps his machine on an even keel by flexing the tips of the planes, much the same as in the Wright model. The tips of the main plane and of the two horizontal rudders are connected with a single lever, which gives the pilot perfect control of them. The horizontal rudders may be turned to steer the aëroplane up or down in the same way. The vertical rudder for turning the aëroplane from right to left, is operated by a foot lever.

The Bleriot monoplane weighs about 500 pounds, so that it carries about four pounds for every square foot of wing surface, or thirteen pounds per square foot, which is from two to four times greater than is the case of any biplane. The machine is mounted on three wheels, two at the front and one near the rear, just forward of the rudders. It has a speed of nearly forty miles an hour.

All the present monoplane models follow the same general plan of placing their propellers and larger planes in front and their horizontal rudder for vertical steering in the rear. The idea is gaining ground, however, that it would be better if this arrangement was reversed, and they flew with what is now the tail in front. The theory of this arrangement is that if the edge of the lifting planes is presented to the air, they would answer the helm much better, as has been proven in the biplane forms. The experiment of reversing the monoplane forms has been tried in model aeroplanes with great success.

The heaviest and largest of the monoplanes at present is the Antoinette model, which is the invention of M. Levasseur. It looks like a great dragon fly, and has proven itself very steady in flight. The main wings, measuring forty-two feet in width seem to be arched unusually high from front to rear, and taper rather sharply at the ends. Their total lifting surface is a trifle over 300 feet. In some of the Antoinette models the wings are set in the form of a broad, dihedral angle. The monoplane is driven from a seat in the body of the frame as the Bleriot model,

A Very Simple Monoplane for Beginners.

but moved slightly farther back. The rear horizontal rudder is controlled by a large wheel at the left of the pilot's seat, while a corresponding wheel on the right controls the small hinged wings at the outer edge of the main plane. The pilot turns his airship from right to left by merely pressing two foot pedals connected with the vertical rudder in the rear. In the later models, the dihedral angle has been abandoned and the front planes set horizontally.

The most novel feature of the Antoinette model is the form and control of the rear rudders and stability planes. The model carries two vertical rudders for turning the craft to the right or left, and a large horizontal rudder for vertical steering, extending far out behind at the end of the main body. All of these rudders are triangular in shape, tapering to a point in the rear. The Antoinette has proved, it is believed, that the corners of square rudders may be removed, without affecting their guiding qualities, thus saving considerable surface and weight. It would seem, on general principles, that just the reverse would be the case. The builder of model aëroplanes may take a leaf from the log of this airship.

The Antoinette stability planes are placed just forward of the rudders, and are triangular in shape, but with somewhat narrow ends pointing toward the front. Two of these planes are carried horizontally and one vertically, the vertical planes being above the horizontals. The chief fault of this model is that the rear horizontal stability plane, being perfectly flat, exerts little lifting power. The method of warping the tips of the planes, the same as in the Wright aëroplane, works well with this model, and the flights, are as a rule, remarkable steady. The machine lands on wooden skids, carried well forward, connected with the frame by flexible joints. It is supported in the rear by two wheels under the center of the planes.

The Santos Dumont monoplane is, so far, the smallest and lightest monoplane to make a successful flight. It is the aëronautical runabout, and, although it has made no very extended air journeys, it has introduced several interesting features. Its owner has flown several miles across country in his little craft, housed it in an ordinary stable while making a call, and then, starting from the front lawn, flown home again without assistance of any kind. His machine may be counted upon to fly at the rate of about thirty-seven miles an hour. It weighs only 245 pounds without the pilot.

The main plane is set at an angle so that, seen from the front, the wings rise from the center, but later bend down toward the tips. The front or entering edge is also elevated to an unusually high degree, giving it the appearance of a rather flat umbrella. The pilot sits underneath this front plane just below the center. The stability of this plane is maintained by fixing the ends in the usual manner. The wires connecting with the ends of the planes, are carried to a lever which is attached to the pilot's back. The pilot, therefore, without using his hands, but merely by swaying his body from side to side, can warp the planes and bring his craft to an even keel.

The Santos Dumont monoplane carries no regular stability plane at the rear, but depends for its support and guidance upon a small vertical and horizontal rudder at the end of its very short frame. These two rudders bisect one another, or in other words, half of the vertical rudder is above and half below the horizontal rudder, while half of the horizontal rudder is on one side and half on the other of the vertical rudder. They are attached to a single rigid framework, so that both move as a whole by means of a universal joint. The rudders, used for ascending and descending, are operated by a lever, while the rudders used for horizontal steering are controlled by a wheel.

The aëroplane is mounted on two wheels, placed at the front of the frame and a vertical strut at the rear, thus re-

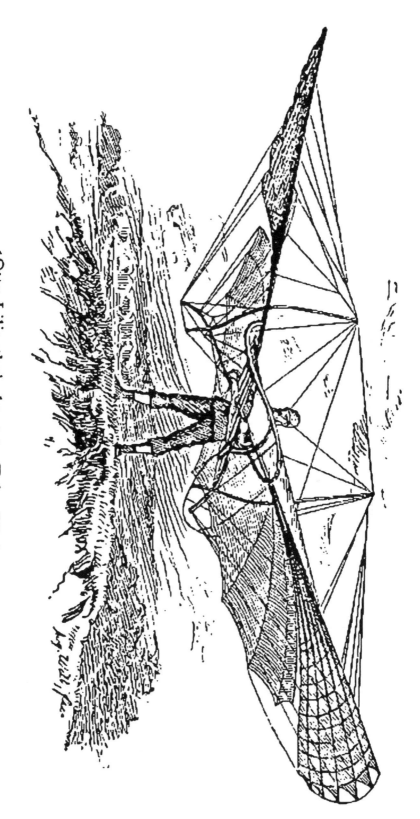

'Otto Lilienthal about to Take Flight.

versing the arrangement of the Antoinette. This adjustment works well in practice, and the Santos Dumont holds the record for rising from the ground in the shortest distance. It has risen in six and a quarter seconds after traveling only 230 feet. The area of its wings is only 110 square feet and its propeller consisting of double wooden blades measures only six feet three inches in diameter. It carries a 30 H. P. motor.

The R. E. P. monoplane, the name being formed by the initials of its inventor, Robert Esnault-Pelterie, is an experiment along new lines. Its inventor believes that the wires and struts of the monoplane in vibrating, offer considerable resistance to the air and seriously retard its forward movement. His monoplane has, therefore, been constructed practically without stays, wires, or rods. The monoplane is graceful in form, light and compact, although somewhat expensive to build.

The main frame of the airship is made of steel girders with a broad surface and tapering to a sharp edge at the bottom. It is covered completely with cloth, thus forming a vertical stability plane of considerable area. The motor and propeller are carried at the front of the frame, while the pilot's seat is fixed inside the frame, just back of the machinery.

The main planes have a span of thirty-five feet six inches. They extend from either side of the frame, and taper slightly toward their outer edges. Two large rudders are carried at the rear of the frame. The vertical rudder for horizontal steering is attached to an extension of the main frame and the horizontal rudder projects from the end at a higher level. A fixed vertical stability plane or fin extends along the main frame back of the pilot's seat. The warping of the plane and the control of both rudders is accomplished by levers placed convenient to the pilot's hand.

The R. E. P. model, alone among the aëroplanes, is equipped with a four blade propeller. It measures six feet six inches in diameter, and is driven at the speed of

1400 revolutions per minute. The speed of the craft is remarkable since it has flown for short distances at the rate of forty-seven miles an hour. Its weight, 780 pounds, is not unusual.

An entirely new idea has been introduced in mounting this model. It rests upon only two wheels, one at the front, the other at the end of the central frame. Wheels are also attached to the outer edges of the main plane. When at rest, the model tilts over to one side or the other and rests on one of these wheels. Once the motor has been started, the machine quickly rights itself, as the speed increases, and runs along on two wheels.

CHAPTER VII

THE boys who turn these pages may some day read of aërial battles fought high above the earth, and some may even take part in them. Air-ships are even now included in the navies of nineteen nations. There is great difference of opinion among experts whether the balloon or aëroplane will prove the better fighting machine, but, meanwhile, aëronautical corps and regiments are being recruited, formidable navies of air-ships are being laid down, and special guns are being built to battle against them.

The ordinary balloon has played a much more important part in actual warfare than most people realize. A balloon corps was organized in France as early as 1794, when balloons were built for each of the

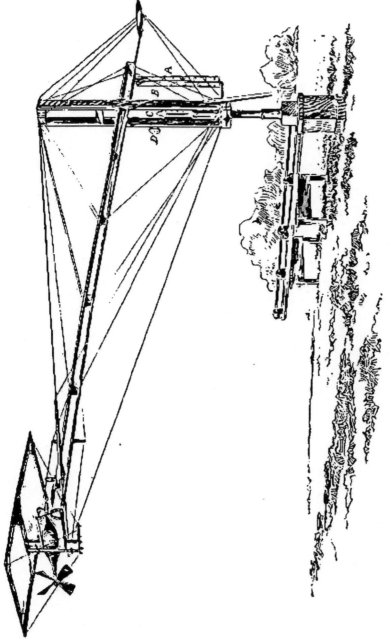

A Machine for Testing the Lifting Power of Aëroplanes.

In this machine power is transmitted from the horizontal main shaft and upward through the vertical steel spindle and through the two members of the long arm. A is a scale showing miles per hour and B a scale divided into feet per minute; C, Dynamometer for recording the push of screw; D, Dynamometer showing the lift of the aeroplane.

Republican armies. One of these balloons, measuring thirty feet in diameter, was sent up near Mayence, to gain a view of the Austrian army. The balloon was held captive by two ropes, and an officer in the car wrote his observations, weighted the letters, and dropped them overboard. The Austrians were furious at this spying, and opened fire, but the ropes were lengthened and the balloon rose to a height of 1300 feet, where it was out of range. Several years later balloons were again used in battles by the French against the Austrians, who were so angry with the new machine that they declared that any balloonist captured would be shot. For a long time afterward, however, this method of warfare was neglected, and even Napoleon could not see its value, and closed the aëronautical school and disbanded the corps.

The use of the balloon was revived in America during the Civil War, and proved to be so valuable that no great war has since been fought without it. During the attack on Richmond, a number of balloons were sent up daily by the Federal Army to overlook the besieged city. From a point eight miles away, valuable information was gained as to the position of the troops and the earthworks. A telegraph apparatus was taken up and messages were sent directly from the clouds, almost over Richmond to Washington.

In the Spanish-American War in 1898, the balloon was again called into use. One ascent was made before Santiago, Cuba, and the position of the various Spanish forces were observed and reported. Another was sent up at El Paso, less than 2000 feet from the Spanish trenches, and the position of the Spanish troops on San Juan Hill was discovered. The balloon was finally brought down by the Spanish guns.

During the siege of Paris in 1870, balloons were used successfully to escape from the city. Some sixty-six of them, carrying 168 passengers, succeeded in passing over the German armies. The

French army has also made good use of the balloon in the wars in Madagascar, and several English balloon corps were engaged with the British army during the Boer War.

For ordinary military work, balloons of three sizes are used, a large balloon for forts, the regular war balloon, and an auxiliary for field work. The large balloon holds 34,500 cubic feet of gas and is only used above fortifications. The regular field balloon is thirty-three feet in diameter, and holds 19,000 cubic feet of gas. It is designed to carry two passengers to a height of 1650 feet. The auxiliary balloon is considerably smaller, holding only 9200 cubic feet of gas, and carrying but one passenger. It is much easier to handle on long marches, and, of course, may be filled and sent aloft in much less time.

The balloons are usually filled from cylinders, which may be hurried across country in carts or automobiles. There is, besides, a regular field gas generator, readily packed up and carried about, which will fill an ordinary balloon in from fifteen to twenty minutes. To resist aërial attacks, a special armored automobile has been adopted by some European armies, carrying a gun which may be aimed upward and at any angle. Despite its weight, the automobile will travel at the rate of forty miles an hour. The recent developments of the dirigible war balloon has rendered the free balloon practically obsolete, and it is unlikely that it will ever again be used in actual warfare.

The United States has been the first country to adopt the aëroplane as a weapon of warfare. After the successful flights of the Wright Brothers, the War Department purchased one of their aëroplanes, and several officers were instructed in driving it. Before being accepted, the Wrights were required to make a flight of ten miles over a rough, mountainous country near Washington, and return without alighting. The test, which was highly successful, was witnessed by President

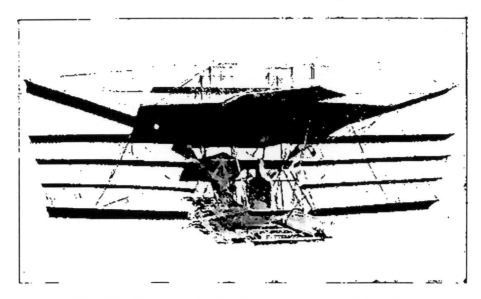

The Machine on the Rails, as it appeared in 1893.

Maxim's First Aëroplane.

Taft and many representatives of the Government. In the event of war, the United States Government could quickly mobilize a formidable fleet of aëroplanes, and man them with experienced aviators.

The value of aëroplanes in warfare has been widely discussed by military experts. There was, at first, a general impression that such flights were much too uncertain to be of practical value. The marvellous development of the aëroplane, and its remarkable flights over land and sea, have served to silence much of this criticism.

Although an over-sea invasion by a fleet of air-ships would seem to be a danger of the very distant future, the United States Government is already preparing to meet the situation. A remarkable series of tests have been made at the Government Proving Grounds at Sandy Hook, by firing at free balloons as they sailed past the fort. The balloons were sent away at various altitudes, in some cases at a considerable distance from the guns, and again directly above them. The difficulty in hitting such targets was found to be very great. The air craft moves so quickly that it is almost impossible to bring a gun of the ordinary mounting into position. Although the results of the test were closely guarded, it is known that the Government was not satisfied with the defense of New York Harbor, in the event of an aërial invasion, and special guns are being designed to repel such an attack.

The military authorities look very far into the future in their preparations. One of the most interesting of these problems is that of protecting our seacoast, should a fleet of aërial warships be sent against us. One of the plans suggested is to raise a series of captive balloons at regular intervals along the shore. It has been thought that some of these might be held near the earth, while others are allowed to ascend to a great altitude. The lookout in these signal stations could sight the approach of an hostile fleet of air-ships at a great distance, and by means of wireless apparatus warn the country of approaching danger.

Many military experts, who have watched the flights of aëroplanes, have decided that the little craft would also prove an extremely difficult object for the enemy to bring down. Since they travel at upwards of a mile a minute, ordinary guns, as they are now mounted, could not hope to hit them except by a lucky shot. It would be like hunting wild geese with a cannon. At a height of several thousand feet, which they can readily attain, an aëroplane might defy the most formidable batteries in the world. Should a fleet of these little craft be sent against an enemy, many of them would be sure to survive an attack, even if a few should be lost. It does not seem probable that the aëroplane will carry aloft a cannon large enough to do any damage. But they can drop high explosives, with astonishing accuracy, and would do important scout work.

At the present cost of construction, a fleet of one hundred aëroplanes might be

built and put in commission in the field or
sky, for what a single great battleship
would cost. It has been shown, moreover,
that a man can learn to operate an aëroplane in less time than it takes to learn to
ride a bicycle. The Wrights instructed
Lieutenant Lahm to drive one of their
machines in about two hours of actual
flight. The war aëroplanes would call for
great bravery and daring, but who can
doubt that men would be found to serve
their country, if need be, by facing this
appalling danger.

In military language, the modern air-
ships fall into three classes, dreadnaughts,
cruisers and scouts. The dreadnaughts of
the air are the largest dirigible balloons,
such as Zeppelin flies. They will probably be used in aërial warfare in the first
line of battle, and for over-sea work. The
cruisers comprise the dirigibles, such as
have been brought to great perfection in
France. These faster air-ships will rise
higher than the dreadnaughts, and will
probably be used for guarding and scout

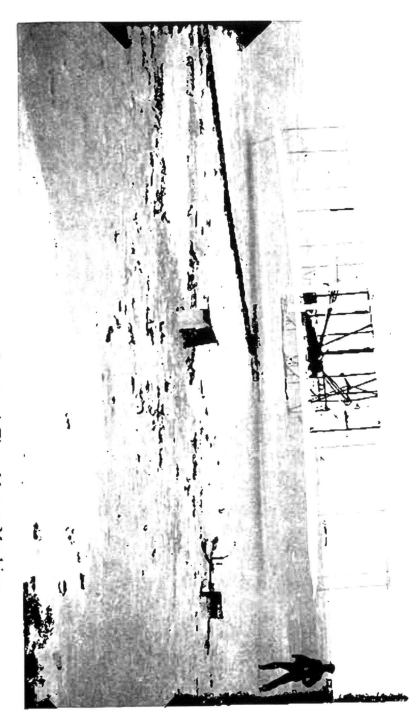

First Flight of the Wright Brothers' First Motor Machine.

This picture shows the machine just after lifting from the track, flying against a wind of twenty-four miles an hour.

work. The aëroplanes come under the head of scouts, and will be used for dispatch work, and for attacking dirigibles.

Their speed and effective radius of travel place the air-ship in the first rank among the engines of war. The value of the free or captive balloon has, of course, been clearly proven. It has been of the greatest value for general observation work in the field. It has been readily raised out of effective range of the enemy's batteries, and from this position, has looked down upon the forts, cities, or encampments. It thus became a signal station which might direct gun fire with absolute accuracy, and has been the only safe and reliable method for locating the presence of mines and submarines.

The dirigible balloon possesses all of the qualities of the free balloon and many more. It can attack by day or night. Its search lights enable it to look down upon the enemy with pitiless accuracy. It may thus gain information about forts and harbors, which otherwise could not be approached. The most completely mined harbor in the world has no terrors for such a visitor. The great problem in warfare of patrolling the frontier of a country against possible invasion seems to be solved by the dirigible. Two or three men aboard a dirigible, with a traveling radius of several hundred miles, could do more effective work than several thousand men scattered along the frontier line.

For dispatch work the flying machine is expected to be indispensable in warfare. The bearer of dispatches has always played an important part in war. His work is often of the most perilous nature, and his journeys, at best, are slow and uncertain. The dispatch bearer, driving an air-ship fifty miles an hour, could ride high above the range of the enemy's guns. These same vehicles of the air would doubtless be equipped with wireless telegraph apparatus, so that they might send or receive messages, and the aviator might talk freely with the entire country side, directing a battery here, silencing one there, ordering an advance or conducting a retreat, with unprecedented accuracy.

These aërial fleets may also carry on deadly aggressive warfare. The over sea raid will have greater terror than any ordinary invasion. A fleet of dreadnaughts dirigibles, assisted by fast cruisers of the air, and many aëroplane scouts, would be extremely formidable. An enemy's base line would be at the mercy of such an invasion. Within a few hours, such a fleet might destroy the enemy's stores, its railroads, and its cities, by dropping explosives or poisonous bombs.

In several recent aëroplane flights, " peace bombs " have been aimed to strike a given mark, and the shots have proven surprisingly accurate. By using various instruments to determine directions, it will be possible to drop such bombs with mathematical accuracy. The bombs or missiles will be suspended by wires from beneath the air-ship and released by an electric current, to give them a perfectly vertical direction. When dropped from great altitudes, the effect of such explosions will be difficult to withstand. Our great war-ships, despite their steel sides, will probably have to be completely re-modelled before they can fight with this new enemy.

When an air-ship drops a bomb from a point directly above a fort or ship, it will be absolutely out of the range of the enemy, since to shoot directly up into the air would be to fire a boomerang which would quickly return and inflict serious damage. An actual test was recently carried out in England, when a thirteen pound gun fired at a balloon 1000 feet in the air. Although the gun had an effective range of 4000 feet, and the balloon was held captive, it was not until the seventeenth shot had been fired that it was brought down. It has also been proven that a rifle ball will be deflected by the draught from the propeller of an aëroplane. The flying machine promises to revolutionize warfare.

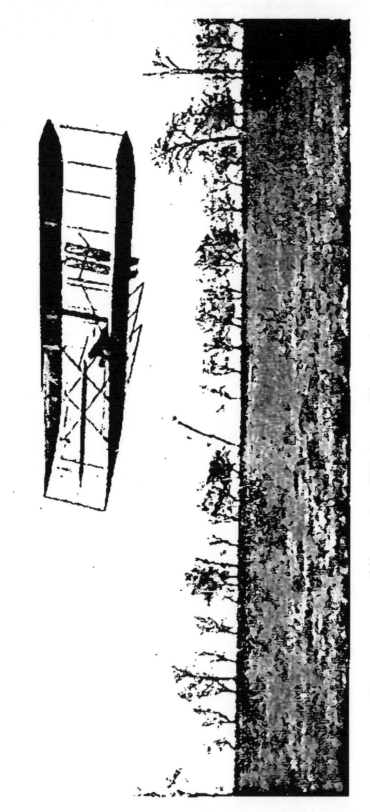

Three-quarters View of a Flight at Simms Station, November 16, 1904

CHAPTER VIII

SPORTS OF THE AIR, AEROPLANES

ANY contest of air-ships makes excellent sport. A city to city flight by aëroplane, for instance, attracts greater crowds than could any procession or royal progress in the past. The aëronautical tournaments and meets already have been held from Egypt in the East, to California in the west. Let an aëroplane soar higher than any has risen before, stay aloft longer, or make a new record for speed or distance, and the news is instantly cabled around the world.

All who have gone aloft tell us that flying is the greatest sport in the world. The free, rapid glide we all enjoy in skating or coasting becomes speedier and smoother in an air-ship, without exerting the least effort. It is this sense of rapid motion which has made the automobile so popular, and the air-ship improves upon the automobile, just as the automobile improved on the lumbering coaches of the past. Once aloft, the aërial passenger glides with the swallow's swiftness. "Now," cried an enthusiastic Frenchwoman, after her first aëroplane flight, "now I understand why the birds sing."

As the aëroplane is brought under better control, we will see these contests grow more and more exciting. The development of the new craft has been so rapid, we have come to expect so much from it, that the exhibition at which the world marvels to-day, becomes the commonplace of to-morrow.

The early flights of the Wright Brothers at Kitty Hawk failed to attract much attention. There had been so many announcements of successful flying machines that many were sceptical, especially in Europe, and the world did not realize that the great day, so long promised, was dawning. It was not till the Wrights flew in North Carolina that the world began to take the matter seriously.

Every movement of the curious new craft was closely watched thereafter. When one of the brothers went aloft the world knew it, and crowds stood patiently before bulletin boards in New York, London, or Sidney, to count the minutes. When he succeeded in staying aloft for an hour, the waiting crowds in many widely separated cities, broke into simultaneous cheers. Next came the trip to Paur, in France, and other European cities, and day by day the flights became longer and higher. The brothers made double progress, for while one was in Southern Europe increasing the time aloft, the other was flying higher and higher in Germany. In these early days no attempt was made to fly across the country. The aëroplane merely flew around and around some large field, and the distance traversed was calculated more or less accurately.

After the triumphant return of the

Wrights to America, a cross-country run was made at Fort Myer, to show the Government that the aëroplane was more than a toy. A flight of twenty miles was made over a rough, mountainous country and several deep valleys. The air of the valleys drew the machine down with a dangerous rush, but the aviator pluckily worked his way higher, and passed over it in safety.

Shortly after this, during the Hudson-Fulton Celebration in New York, Mr. Wilbur Wright rose from Governor's Island in New York harbor, encircled the Statue of Liberty, and again sailed high above the river north to Grant's Tomb, and returned to the starting point. Each of these feats was, in a peculiar sense, record breaking.

Meanwhile, a flock of aviators were making ascensions in biplanes and monoplanes of many designs in France. Their first attempts to fly were made, as a rule, in a great field on the outskirts of Paris, where immense crowds gathered to watch them. As the aviators gained confidence in their craft, the flights rapidly became

Front View of the Flight of the Wright Aëroplane, October 4, 1905.

longer and higher, and short cross-country flights were made. These cross-country and over-water flights quickly out-distanced those made in America, and this lead once gained, was kept up. There are several reasons why France, after America pointed the way, should have overtaken, and, in some respects, out-distanced her. There have been more aviators in France. The prizes offered for flights of various kinds, have been ten times more numerous and valuable in France than in any other country, and this naturally invited competition. The example of France in offering valuable prizes for long flights has since been followed in the United States.

It should be borne in mind, again, that the level stretches of country common in Europe, offers fewer difficulties for the pilot of the aëroplane than the rough, mountainous, or even hilly country often encountered in America. It is possible to fly hundreds of miles in the south of France or in Italy and pass over country like a great parade ground. When a long-distance flight is made in America, rivalling or surpassing those made abroad, it is probable that it has required far more skill and daring than similar European flights. The French, again, excel in building light, serviceable motors, suitable for aëroplanes, and no small part of the success of the French air craft is due to this skill.

The cross-country trips were quickly extended. After several successful short flights, Henry Farman surpassed all records by traveling for eighty-three miles across country in France. The great feat was now to cross the English Channel. A prize of $5,000 was offered by a London newspaper for the first channel flight. Two attempts were made by a young Frenchman, Hubert Latham, but both times, after sailing out for several miles over the sea, some accident befell his machine, and he was thrown into the water. Undaunted by these failures, another Frenchman, Louis Bleriot, started early one Sunday morning, June 25, 1909, from a point near Calais, France, and landed safely at Dover on the English side. Shortly after this, still another Frenchman, De Lesseps, flew from the French coast to England in safety.

The richest of the aviation prizes, a purse of $50,000, had meanwhile been offered for a successful trip by a heavier-than-air machine from London to Manchester, a distance of 171 miles. Several attempts had been made to cover this distance, but without success. It was finally won, however, under very dramatic circumstances. Two aviators, an Englishman named White and a Frenchman named Paulhan, actually raced for the goal. The French machine got away first, but was followed by the English machine close on his heels — or should we say propellers? The greater part of the race took place at night in a high wind, and, in the upper air lanes, intensely cold weather.

Paulhan succeeded in flying 117 miles without coming down, rushing along through the night at top speed, with the dread that every sound behind him came from the machine of his rival. When he was forced to land for fuel, he worked with feverish haste, fearing that every second's delay might cost him the coveted prize. Several times the crowd about him, deceived by some night bird, cried "Here comes White!" As a matter of fact, White was but a few miles behind. The fuel tank filled, Paulhan drove his machine full speed into the sky, and did not land till he had completed the journey and won the prize.

There was naturally a great demand for a similar journey in America, and the aviator and the prize were soon found. For several years there had been a standing prize of $10,000 for the first successful flight between New York and Albany, over the Hudson River, the course taken by Robert Fulton in his famous trip by steamboat in 1809. An effort was made to cover the distance by dirigible balloon without success. An attempt was made by aëroplane on May, 1910, by Glenn H. Curtiss, the winner of the grand prize for speed in the aviation meeting at Rheims. Curtis started from Albany, in order to face the air currents which drew up the river. After waiting for several days for fair weather, he finally got away early one morning, and, following the course of the Hudson River, made the flight to Poughkeepsie, seventy-five miles south, without mishap, when he landed for fuel.

Again rising into the air, he started south, traveling with such speed, that he outdistanced the special train which was following him. A difficult problem in aviation was met in passing over the Highlands, a rugged mountainous section, through which the river cuts a deep, tortuous channel. Curtiss rose to a height of more than 1000 feet, but the treacherous air currents drew him down and tossed him about at perilous angles. He fought his way, foot by foot, finally bringing his craft to an even keel. On reaching New York, he landed in the upper section of the city for gasolene, and once more rising above the Hudson River, flew swiftly to the riotous clamor of every whistle in the great harbor beneath him, to a safe landing at Governor's Island.

The first great city to city and return aëroplane trip was made a few days later, between New York and Philadelphia. A new aspirant for these honors was Mr. Charles K. Hamilton, who had amazed everyone with his daring driving. He was engaged to fly over the course for $10,000, offered by a New York and a Philadelphia newspaper. He carried with him letters from the Governor of New York and the Mayor of New York City to the Governor of Pennsylvania and the Mayor of Philadelphia. He also took aloft a number of "peace bombs," which he dropped along the route to show how accurate might be the aim of a war aëroplane. The start was made early on the morning of June 13, from Governor's Island in New York harbor. A special train was held in readiness to follow him.

After rising to a considerable altitude, Hamilton flew in great circles about the

island to try his wings, and then, signaling
that all was ready, darted off to the south.
He quickly picked up his special train, and,
at a pace of almost a mile a minute, flying
hundreds of feet in air, sped on to Philadelphia. It was estimated that more than
1,000,000 people had gathered along the
route to cheer him. Hamilton had laid out
a regular time-table before starting, and
so perfect was his control of the machine,
that he passed town after town on time
to the minute like a railroad train.

The run to Philadelphia eighty miles
away, was made without alighting and
without mishap of any kind. Hamilton
flew over the open field selected for landing, circled it three times to show that he
was not tired in the least, and settled down
as lightly as a bird. He was received by
the Governor of Pennsylvania and the
Deputy Mayor of Philadelphia, to whom
he delivered his messages and received
similar letters in reply to bring back to
New York.

After a brief rest of little more than one

hour, Hamilton was once more in the sky, flying across-country at express speed. He set such a pace, that his special train was left far behind, and it was only by running at the rate of seventy-five miles an hour, that it finally overtook him. Hamilton drew far ahead of the train on the return trip which was made in much faster time. The wind was favorable, and Newark, eighty miles, was reached at the rate of fifty miles an hour.

With the goal practically in sight, Hamilton's engine began working badly. He pushed on, until he found himself in absolute danger, when he decided to descend. From such high altitudes, the appearance of the ground is very deceptive. Hamilton chose what appeared to be a smooth piece of green grass and dropped to it, only to discover that he had settled in a marsh. The fault in the engine was quickly remedied, but now the ground proved too soft for him to rise. In trying to rise he broke his propeller, and another delay followed, while a new propeller was hurried from New York. He finally succeeded, however, in rising and completing his trip to Governor's Island, thus making the round trip in a day and winning the prize.

So rapid is the advance in the new science, that each aviation meet sets a new and more difficult standard. At first, people marvelled to see an aëroplane rising but a few feet from the ground, but such feats soon became commonplace. Within a few months, prizes were offered for the machine staying aloft for the longest time. The element of speed was next considered, and the aëroplanes sailed around a race course against time. The highest altitude now became a popular test feat. The pilots soon found themselves in such complete control of their machines that they gave exhibitions of landing by the force of gravity alone. The aëroplane would work its way upward in great spirals, and then, shutting off all power, coast down at terrifying angles on the unsubstantial air. It is from such tests as these that there will gradually evolve the airships of the future, the terrible engines of war, the air liners for commerce, and the light and speedy pleasure craft.

Printed in Great Britain
by Amazon.co.uk, Ltd.,
Marston Gate.